CHICKEN

CHICKEN

hamlyn

Published in the UK in 1998
by Hamlyn, a division of Octopus Publishing Group Ltd
2–4 Heron Quays, London E14 4JP

This edition published 2002 by Octopus Publishing Group Ltd

Copyright ©1998, 2002 Octopus Publishing Group Ltd

ISBN 0 600 60819 0

Printed in China

NOTES

Both metric and imperial measurements have been given in all
recipes. Use one set of measurements only and not a
mixture of both.

Standard level spoon measurements are used in all recipes.
1 tablespoon = one 15 ml spoon
1 teaspoon = one 5 ml spoon

Eggs should be medium to large unless otherwise stated.
The Department of Health advises that eggs should not be
consumed raw. This book contains dishes made with raw or
lightly cooked eggs. It is prudent for more vulnerable people
such as pregnant and nursing mothers, invalids, the elderly,
babies and young children to avoid uncooked or lightly cooked
dishes made with eggs. Once prepared, these dishes should
be kept refrigerated and used promptly.

Milk should be full fat unless otherwise stated.

Poultry should be cooked thoroughly. To test if poultry is cooked,
pierce the flesh through the thickest part with a skewer or fork –
the juices should run clear, never pink or red.

Do not re-freeze a dish that has been frozen previously.

Pepper should be freshly ground black pepper unless
otherwise stated.

Fresh herbs should be used, unless otherwise stated. If
unavailable, use dried herbs as an alternative but halve the
quantities stated.

Measurements for canned food have been given as a standard
metric equivalent.

Nuts and nut derivatives
This book includes dishes made with nuts and nut derivatives.
It is advisable for customers with known allergic reactions to
nuts and nut derivatives and those who may be potentially
vulnerable to these allergies, such as pregnant and nursing
mothers, invalids, the elderly, babies and children, to avoid
dishes made with nuts and nut oils. It is also prudent to check
the labels of pre-prepared ingredients for the possible inclusion
of nut derivatives.

Ovens should be preheated to the specified temperature – if
using a fan-assisted oven, follow the manufacturer's
instructions for adjusting the time and the temperature.

Contents

Introduction

Delicious, nutritious, readily available and quick and easy to prepare, chicken is, not surprisingly, one of our most popular meats. Its attractive creamy white colour and delicate flavour mean that it can be cooked with an infinite combination of flavourings in dishes which can be as simple or as complicated as the cook likes – or has time to prepare.

CHOOSING CHICKEN

Nowadays, chicken and other poultry take up more space on the supermarket shelves than any other kind of meat, and the cook has a great choice, both in the kinds and cuts of chicken available and the price to be paid for it.

At the top end of the range are organically-reared and free-range birds. Both are succulent and full of flavour but may also be more expensive, since they cannot be reared in the great numbers produced by indoor rearing. Mass-produced chicken also comes in more than one variety. The most notable are the corn-fed or maize-fed chickens, the flesh of which takes on a lovely creamy-yellow colour from the corn fed to the birds. Cheapest of all chickens are the whole birds and joints to be found in the supermarket freezer cabinet. Although frozen chicken does not have quite the same flavour as fresh, it is still very nutritious and can be made into a range of tasty dishes. It is also ideal for making chicken stock.

WHOLE CHICKENS

Whole chickens, usually sold 'oven-ready', which means they have been plucked, drawn and trussed, range in size from the tiny poussin, weighing up to 500 g/1 lb, through spring chickens, weighing about 1.25 kg/2½ lb, up to birds of about 2.75 kg/6 lb. Really large chickens with a high proportion of flavoursome flesh, sometimes called capons and weighing up to 4 kg/8 lb or so, are also available, especially around Christmas time from butchers or game dealers and make a good alternative to the Christmas turkey.

Whole chickens may be roasted (with or without stuffing), pot-roasted, braised, boiled or steamed. Poussin may be spatchcocked for quick cooking (see page 7). When choosing a whole chicken, look for one with a plump, white breast, smooth and pliable legs, a pliable breastbone, and moist, but not wet, skin which is free of dark patches and has not split.

CHICKEN PIECES

Ready-jointed chicken is available in quarters (including leg and breast meat, with bones in), breasts, thighs and drumsticks, the last two being cheaper than breasts and excellent for casseroling, stewing, and barbecuing.

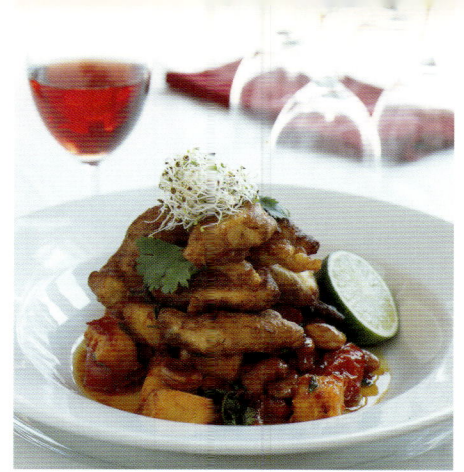

Chicken breasts, which are the leanest and most delicately-flavoured parts of the bird, are available with or without bones and skin. Suprêmes are a speciality cut, which have the breast bone removed but part of the wing bone left on. Boneless breasts may be sold as 'fillets' or, when sliced or pounded, as 'escalopes'. Whatever its shape or size, chicken breast meat lends itself to quick cooking, using methods such as grilling, stir-frying, poaching and barbecuing.

CHICKEN GIBLETS

Supermarket chickens are usually sold without their giblets, so if you want them, perhaps to add to a stock or gravy, you may have to go to a proper butcher. Chicken livers are a different matter. Widely available, both fresh and frozen, they make excellent pâtés and terrines, and dishes such as warm chicken liver salads are increasingly popular. They also go well with alcohol flavourings, in dishes which can be prepared in minutes: see the recipe for Livers Oporto on page 45.

PREPARING CHICKEN

Raw poultry contains low levels of bacteria, especially salmonella, which can cause food poisoning, but which careful storage, proper handling and thorough cooking will eliminate. Fresh raw poultry should be put in the refrigerator as soon as it is brought home. Packing such as plastic bags and polystyrene trays should be removed and the chicken put on a plate and covered with foil. If you have bought a whole chicken with giblets, take them out of the bird and store them separately in a covered bowl. All fresh chicken should be prepared and eaten within two days.

Frozen chicken should be put in the freezer immediately you get it home. Before cooking, it must be thawed completely at a cool room temperature so that no ice crystals remain. If the chicken is being thawed in a microwave, scrupulously observe the instructions in the microwave's handbook. Do not thaw frozen chicken by putting it in hot water, since all you will achieve is toughened flesh. Never refreeze thawed raw chicken.

Before preparing raw chicken, make sure that hands, chopping boards and utensils are all clean. Once you have finished, thoroughly wash them all again.

The one essential piece of equipment you will need when preparing a chicken is a large kitchen knife, which must be both very sharp and clean. Other helpful tools are a small sharp knife for boning, and poultry shears. Once the chicken is cooked, it may need to be carved, and the carving knife should also be very sharp, since a blunt knife will tend to squash the meat instead of slicing quickly through it, and allow the juices to be forced out.

JOINTING A CHICKEN

Several recipes in this book require a whole chicken, cut into pieces. The usual number of pieces into which a chicken is divided is eight, though bigger ones may have breasts large enough to cut into two pieces each. To joint a chicken:

1 Place the chicken on a clean chopping board. Pull one leg away from the body and twist it sharply to break the thigh joint. Use a sharp knife to cut the leg away from the body. If the leg is large enough, cut it in two through the knee joint, to give a drumstick and a thigh. Repeat with the second leg.

2 Cut down from the base of the breast towards a wing joint and cut the wing away from the body, leaving some breast meat attached. Cut off and discard the wing tip. Repeat with the other wing.

3 Cut along one side of the top of the rib cage to separate the remainder of the breast meat from the carcass. Repeat with the other breast.

4 Use the carcass to make stock.

QUARTERING A SMALL CHICKEN

1 Place the bird on a chopping board and, using a sharp knife or poultry shears, cut it lengthways down through the breastbone and then through the backbone underneath.

2 Cut through the two halves, to give four quarters.

SPATCHCOCKING A POUSSIN

A spatchcocked poussin looks impressive and cooks quickly, making it great for barbecues. Although spatchcocked poussin has become a regular item on supermarket shelves, there is no reason why this relatively simple job cannot be done at home. As well as the usual sharp knife, you will need one pair of long skewers per bird. If using wooden skewers, soak them in water for 30 minutes before use to prevent them burning during cooking.

1 Put the poussin, breast down, on a chopping board. Cut along each side of the backbone (poultry shears are ideal for this) and discard it.

2 Open out the bird and cut the wishbone in half. Turn the bird over so that it is breast up on the board and push down on it with the heel of your hand to break the breastbone and flatten it.

3 Trim off the ends of the wings. Cut a slit in the skin between the breastbone and each leg and tuck the ends of the legs into the slits.

4 To keep the bird flat as it cooks, thread the skewers across the bird through both wings and legs. Wipe the bird with absorbent kitchen paper.

COOKING CHICKEN

Thorough cooking is essential to make the bacteria which are present in raw poultry harmless. All the recipes in this book have cooking times which have been carefully checked to ensure thorough cooking. Follow the instructions and you will have perfectly-cooked food, safe for everyone in the family.

Chicken is relatively low in fat, with much of the fat in it being found in the skin. Because of this, some people remove all the skin before cooking. But the skin does help keep the flesh moist and succulent, especially during roasting, grilling and barbecuing, so you may prefer to cook the chicken with its skin on and remove it before serving.

To test that a whole chicken is cooked, insert a skewer into the thickest part of the thigh. If the juices run clear, the chicken is cooked; any hint of pinkness in the juices means that more cooking is needed.

ROASTING CHICKEN

Roasting is the simplest way of cooking a whole chicken. An open pan is used for roasting, since covering the pan would mean the chicken would be partly cooked in steam – in other words, it would be pot-roasted or braised. The chicken is roasted in the centre of a preheated oven.

A good quality, fresh chicken needs very little attention before roasting: just a shake of salt and pepper over it, a sprinkling of herbs, such as tarragon, oregano or thyme, plus, if you are not barding it with bacon or covering it with foil, 2–3 tablespoons of vegetable oil drizzled over the top. For a fresh flavour, squeeze half a lemon over the bird and put the squeezed skin into the cavity before roasting.

Since chicken is roasted on its back, its tender breast meat should be protected for most of the cooking time. Either lay strips of fatty bacon over the chicken or cover it lightly with foil, removing either about 15 minutes before the end of cooking time to allow the breast to brown and crisp. Alternatively, baste the chicken with the pan juices at regular intervals during cooking to keep it moist.

Roasting times and temperatures for whole chickens are as follows.

For birds weighing up to 1.75 kg/3½ lb, allow 20 minutes per 500 g/1 lb, plus 20 minutes extra at 190°C (375°F), Gas Mark 5.

For birds weighing 2–3 kg/4–6 lb, allow 25 minutes per 500 g/1 lb, plus 25 minutes extra at 160°C (325°F), Gas Mark 3.

Extra care is needed when roasting a stuffed chicken. It is best to stuff only the neck end of larger chickens, since any stuffing in the cavity could draw up bacteria from the raw juices, while the stuffing could prevent the centre of the bird being thoroughly cooked. A stuffed bird, whatever its size, is best roasted at a moderate or moderately hot temperature. Too cool an oven could allow any bacteria in the stuffing to remain active, while too hot a temperature could mean the bird being in the oven too short a time to cook right through the stuffing.

CHICKEN STOCK

Chicken stock is used in soups, stews and casseroles. The recipe below is suitable for all these, and many more.

1 whole chicken carcass

1 teaspoon salt

1 Spanish onion, peeled and stuck with

4 cloves

2 celery sticks, chopped

2 carrots, coarsely chopped

2 parsley sprigs

1 bouquet garni

1 bay leaf

8 black peppercorns

1 Put the carcass into a deep saucepan, cover with 3.4 litres/6 pints water and add the salt. Bring to the boil, skimming off the scum with a slotted spoon. Lower the heat, partially cover the pan and simmer for 1 hour.
2 Add the onion, celery, carrots, parsley, bouquet garni, bay leaf and peppercorns. Stir and continue simmering, partially covered, for a further 1½–2 hours. Add more water if the level drops below the bones.
3 Cool slightly. Remove the carcass, then strain the stock through a fine sieve into a bowl, discarding all the vegetables and herbs. After straining the stock, pick over the carcass, remove any meat still on the bones and add it to the stock.
4 Leave to cool, then skim off the fat with a spoon or blot with kitchen paper. Cover the stock, refrigerate it and use within 3 days. This stock is suitable for freezing; if frozen use within 3 months.

PRESENTATION IDEAS

As the photographs in this book show, an attractive garnish can turn even the simplest recipe into a memorable dish. Many of the garnishes used in this book are based on fresh ingredients, such as herbs, fruits and vegetables,

often in tandem with items like croûtons or roasted chopped nuts.

• **Fresh herbs** Herbs which can be used to garnish chicken dishes include tarragon, mint, parsley, basil, oregano, thyme and coriander. All of these will grow successfully in pots, perhaps on the kitchen windowsill. Always wash herbs and dry them on absorbent kitchen paper before use. Large-leafed herbs can be crisply fried to make a garnish with a difference: see the recipe for Crispy Basil on page 31.

• **Spring onions** These can be cut and sliced in many ways to make garnishes for all kinds of dishes, though they are particularly appropriate for oriental dishes. Smaller spring onions, trimmed, make an impressive garnish if left whole. Other spring onion garnishes include slices, made either straight across or diagonally; the diagonal slices can be quite large, as on the Chilli Chicken with Pine Nuts (see page 38). Spring onion tassels, a favourite of Chinese restaurants, are made by trimming the spring onion, then carefully cutting about 5 cm/2 inches down from the top of the onion

to form delicate fronds; drop the spring onion into iced water to allow the tassels to open. Spring Onion Fans (see page 52) are a variation on the tassel in which both ends of the onion are cut.

• **Red chillies** These make colourful garnishes for hot and spicy dishes. Slice them finely across to make delicate rings; for less hot chilli rings, cut the chilli open down one side and carefully remove the seeds before slicing them. For chilli flowers, slice the chilli open along one side and remove the seeds, then cut down from the top to make fronds, as for the spring onion tassels above. Remember always to wash your hands thoroughly after you have been handling chillies and never to touch your face or eyes until you have done so.

• **Citrus fruits** Oranges, lemons and limes all make splendid garnishes. Fine slices and wedges are easy but effective citrus fruit garnishes. Make twists by cutting into the centre of a slice then twisting the edges away from each other. Strips of zest, cut with a paring knife or vegetable peeler,

also look good. An attractive way of serving something as large as half a lemon as a garnish is to pare away a ring of zest from the cut edge, leaving it attached on one side, then pulling up the zest into a twist: this is one of the garnishes used for Chicken with Cream Cheese, Garlic and Herbs (see page 40). See the photographs above which show how to do this.

• **Nuts** Peanuts, flaked almonds and chopped walnuts are all used as garnishes for dishes in this book, but other kinds of nuts could be used. For a stronger flavour, roast the nuts by dry-frying or grilling until they colour. Turn frequently to prevent burning.

Soups, Snacks and Salads

The delicate flavour of chicken allows it to be prepared in a wide variety of ways. Using tasty ingredients ranging from exotic Indonesian spices to familiar fruits and vegetables, you can create a range of sumptuous dishes; from rich soups for the winter to delicious salads in the summer, and a delightful snack in between.

Harira

A thick Moroccan soup, wholesome and rich in flavour.

Preparation time: about 25 minutes, plus soaking
Cooking time: about 2¾ hours

- 250 g/8 oz chickpeas, soaked in cold water overnight
- 2 chicken breasts, halved
- 1.2 litres/2 pints Chicken Stock (see page 8)
- 1.2 litres/2 pints water
- 2 x 400 g/13 oz cans chopped tomatoes
- ¼ teaspoon crumbled saffron threads (optional)
- 2 onions, chopped
- 125 g/4 oz white long-grain rice
- 50 g/2 oz green lentils
- 2 tablespoons finely chopped coriander
- 2 tablespoons finely chopped parsley
- salt and pepper
- coriander sprigs, to garnish
- natural yogurt, to serve

1 Drain the chickpeas in a colander, rinse under cold running water and drain again. Place them in a saucepan, cover with 5 cm/2 inches of water and bring to the boil. Lower the heat and simmer, partially covered, until tender, adding more water as necessary. This will take anything up to *2 hours*. Drain the chickpeas and set aside.

2 Combine the chicken breasts, stock and water in a second saucepan. Bring to the boil, lower the heat, cover the pan and simmer for *10–15 minutes* or until the chicken is just cooked. Remove the chicken from the stock, place it on a board and shred it, discarding the skin and any bones. Set the shredded chicken aside.

3 Add the chickpeas, tomatoes, saffron (if using), onions, rice and lentils to the stock remaining in the pan. Simmer, covered, for *30–35 minutes*, or until the rice and lentils are tender.

4 Just before serving, add the shredded chicken, coriander and parsley. Heat the soup for a further *5 minutes* without letting it boil. Season with salt and pepper. Serve garnished with coriander sprigs and drizzled with natural yogurt.

Serves 8–10

Cream of Chicken Soup

Preparation time: 15 minutes
Cooking time: 1¼ hours

- 1 chicken carcass
- 1 onion
- 1 bouquet garni
- 1.2 litres/2 pints Chicken
  Stock (see page 8)
- 125 g/4 oz cooked chicken
- 300 ml/½ pint milk
- 50 g/2 oz plain flour
- 2 tablespoons water

- 1 tablespoon lemon juice
- ¼ teaspoon grated nutmeg
- salt and pepper
- 150 ml/¼ pint single cream
- ½ lemon, to serve

TO GARNISH:
- croûtons
- flat leaf parsley
- grated nutmeg

1 Simmer the carcass, onion and bouquet garni in the stock for about *1 hour*. Strain the liquid and return it to the saucepan.

2 Neatly dice the cooked chicken meat. Add the chicken meat and milk to the stock. Blend the flour with the water, then slowly add the mixture to the stock, stirring all the time. Bring to the boil, then reduce the heat and simmer gently for *10 minutes*. Season the soup with lemon juice, nutmeg, and salt and pepper.

3 To serve, pour the soup into individual soup bowls, pour over the cream and garnish with croûtons, flat leaf parsley and some grated nutmeg. Serve with lemon on the side.

Serves 6

variation
Chicken and Mushroom Soup

Preparation time: 15 minutes
Cooking time: 1¼ hours

1 Finely chop 125 g/4 oz of open cap mushrooms and fry in 25 g/1 oz butter over a moderate heat until lightly browned.

2 Follow the main recipe to make the soup, adding the fried mushrooms to the pan with the chopped chicken.

Serves 6

Creamy Corn and Chicken Chowder

Preparation time: 15 minutes
Cooking time: about 30 minutes

- 25 g/1 oz butter or
  margarine
- 1 large onion, chopped
- 1 small red pepper, cored,
  deseeded and diced
- 625 g/1¼ lb potatoes, diced
- 25 g/1 oz plain flour
- 750 ml/1¼ pints Chicken
  Stock (see page 8)
- 175 g/6 oz sweetcorn
  kernels
- 250 g/8 oz cooked chicken,
  chopped
- 450 ml/¾ pint milk
- 3 tablespoons chopped
  parsley
- salt and pepper
- red chillies, sliced, to
  garnish

1 Melt the butter or margarine in a large saucepan. Add the onion, red pepper and potatoes and fry over a moderate heat for *5 minutes*, stirring from time to time.

2 Sprinkle in the flour and cook over a gentle heat for *1 minute*. Gradually stir in the stock and bring to the boil, stirring, then lower the heat, cover and cook for *10 minutes*.

3 Stir in the sweetcorn, chicken, milk, parsley, and salt and pepper to taste, then cover and simmer gently for a further *10 minutes* until the potatoes are just tender. Taste and adjust the seasoning.

4 Serve the chowder hot in warmed soup bowls, garnished with the sliced chillies.

Serves 4–6

Gado Gado with Chicken

This version of the Indonesian salad has shredded cooked chicken added with all the vegetables.

Preparation time: 30 minutes
Cooking time: 1–2 minutes

- 250 g/8 oz carrots, cut into matchsticks
- 175 g/6 oz celery, cut into matchsticks
- 175 g/6 oz leek, cut into matchsticks
- 125 g/4 oz mangetout
- ½ cucumber, peeled and cut in half lengthways
- 175 g/6 oz bean sprouts
- 175 g/6 oz pak choi or other oriental leaves
- 2 cooked chicken breasts, skinned and shredded
- 1 quantity Spicy Peanut Dressing
- salt and pepper
- chopped fresh coriander, to garnish (optional)

1 Bring a saucepan of water to the boil, add the carrot, celery and leek matchsticks and blanch for *1–2 minutes*. Drain in a colander, refresh under cold running water, and then drain again thoroughly. Tip into a large bowl.

2 Cut the mangetout in half diagonally. Using a teaspoon, scoop out the seeds from the cucumber and cut the flesh into slices.

3 Add the mangetout, cucumber and bean sprouts to the bowl. Season with salt and pepper. Gently toss all the vegetables together to mix.

4 Arrange the pak choi leaves on a serving platter or individual plates, with the shredded chicken and the vegetable mixture. Spoon over the dressing. Garnish with a sprinkling of chopped coriander, if liked.

Serves 4

Spicy Peanut Dressing

Make this rich spicy dressing a little in advance to allow the flavours to develop before using. It is the perfect dressing for Gado Gado, but it is also delicious with plain grilled chicken.

Preparation time: 10 minutes
Cooking time: 2 minutes

- 25 g/1 oz creamed coconut
- 4 tablespoons milk
- ½ small onion, chopped
- 1 garlic clove, crushed
- 4 tablespoons smooth peanut butter
- 1 teaspoon soft light brown sugar
- 2 teaspoons soy sauce
- ½ teaspoon ground cumin
- ½ teaspoon chilli powder
- salt and pepper

1 Chop the creamed coconut and place it in a small saucepan with the milk. Heat gently for about *2 minutes*, stirring, until the coconut melts and forms a paste with the milk.

2 Transfer the coconut mixture to a liquidizer or food processor. Add all the remaining ingredients, with salt and pepper to taste, and purée until smooth, then scrape into a small bowl. Cover and set aside until required.

Serves 4

Nasi Goreng

This famous Indonesian rice dish can be made with other meats besides chicken. Duck or turkey breasts can be used, or pork or beef, or a mixture of different meats.

Preparation time: 15 minutes
Cooking time: about 30 minutes

- 375 g/12 oz long-grain rice
- 2 eggs
- 2 tablespoons oil
- 1 small onion, finely chopped
- 2 garlic cloves, roughly chopped
- 1 red chilli, deseeded and roughly chopped
- 500 g/1 lb skinless, boneless chicken breast, cut diagonally into thin strips
- 250 g/8 oz cooked peeled prawns
- about 2 tablespoons soy sauce
- salt and pepper
- spring onions, to garnish
- prawn crackers, to serve

1 Rinse the rice under cold running water, put it in a large saucepan and cover with cold water. Bring to the boil with 1 teaspoon salt, stir well, then lower the heat and simmer, uncovered, for *20 minutes* or until rice is tender. Drain, rinse under cold running water, and drain again thoroughly. Set aside to cool.

2 To make an omelette, beat the eggs lightly, adding a little salt and pepper to taste. Heat 1½ teaspoons of the oil in a small frying pan until it is hot but not smoking. Pour the eggs over the base of the pan, lift up the edges and let the unset egg run underneath. Cook until the underneath is golden and the top set. Slide the omelette out of pan, then roll it up carefully into a cigar shape. Leave the omelette to cool, seam side down.

3 Crush the onion, garlic and chilli into a paste, then fry in the remaining oil in a wok or large, deep frying pan for about *1–2 minutes* until fragrant. Add chicken, and stir-fry for *3–4 minutes* until it changes colour on all sides. Add the prawns and the soy sauce. Stir-fry until the chicken is tender.

4 Mix the cold rice with the chicken and prawns in the wok. Toss over a high heat until the rice is piping hot. Add salt, pepper and more soy sauce to taste, if required.

5 Turn the rice mixture into a serving dish and garnish with spring onions and the omelette, cut into thin rings. Serve with prawn crackers.

Serves 4–6

Hot Chicken and Walnut Salad

Preparation time: 30 minutes
Cooking time: 12 minutes

- 125 g/4 oz mangetout, halved
- about 250 g/8 oz mixed salad leaves (such as red oakleaf, batavia, frisée, radicchio)
- ½ red onion, thinly sliced
- 3 skinless, boneless chicken breasts
- 3 tablespoons olive oil
- 3 tablespoons walnut oil
- 1 garlic clove, crushed
- 2 tablespoons sherry vinegar or wine vinegar
- 50 g/2 oz walnut pieces
- rind of 1 lemon, cut into thin strips
- 1 teaspoon soft light brown sugar
- salt and pepper
- handful of parsley sprigs, to garnish (optional)

1 Bring a saucepan of water to the boil, add the mangetout and blanch for *1 minute*. Drain in a colander, refresh under cold running water, and drain again thoroughly.

2 Tear the salad leaves into bite-sized pieces. Arrange with the mangetout and the onion around the edge of a large serving platter or individual plates.

3 Cut the chicken breasts into thick slices and, using a rolling pin, flatten the slices between 2 sheets of greaseproof paper or clingfilm to give thin medallions.

4 Heat the olive oil in a large frying pan. Add the chicken pieces, a few at a time and cook over a high heat for about *2 minutes*, turning once, until lightly browned and cooked through. Using tongs, transfer the medallions to a plate and keep warm while cooking the remaining chicken pieces.

5 When all the chicken pieces are cooked, add the walnut oil to the oil remaining in the pan. Stir in the remaining ingredients, with salt and pepper to taste. Heat through, stirring, then return the chicken to the pan. Toss the chicken pieces in the hot dressing to coat.

6 Pile the hot chicken mixture in the centre of the salad leaves. Serve at once, scattered with torn parsley leaves, if liked.

Serves 4

Tarragon and Thyme Chicken Salad

This deliciously simple chicken salad recipe uses a tasty herb mustard. If you cannot buy tarragon and thyme mustard, then add a little chopped fresh tarragon and thyme to your favourite mustard.

Preparation time: 20–30 minutes

- 2 kg/4 lb chicken, roasted
- 4 celery sticks, sliced
- 1 red dessert apple, cored and chopped
- 1 green pepper, cored, deseeded and chopped
- ½ round lettuce, separated into leaves
- 25 g/1 oz slivered almonds, toasted

TO GARNISH:
- tarragon leaves
- celery leaves

DRESSING:
- 4 tablespoons mayonnaise
- 4 tablespoons soured cream
- 2 tablespoons tarragon and thyme mustard
- salt and pepper

1 Remove the skin from the cold roast chicken and chop the meat into bite-sized pieces. Place it in a bowl with the celery, apple and green pepper.

2 To make the dressing, mix the mayonnaise with the soured cream, mustard and salt and pepper to taste. Fold into the chicken mixture to coat evenly.

3 Line individual serving plates with the lettuce leaves and top with the chicken mixture. Sprinkle with the toasted almonds and garnish with tarragon and celery leaves. Serve lightly chilled.

Serves 4–6

variation
Curried Chicken Salad

Preparation time: 20–30 minutes
Cooking time: 8 minutes

- 2 kg/4 lb chicken, roasted
- ½ round lettuce, separated into leaves
- 25 g/1 oz slivered almonds, toasted

DRESSING:
- 1 tablespoon oil
- 1 small onion, chopped
- 1 tablespoon mild curry powder
- 150 ml/¼ pint Chicken Stock (see page 8)
- 2 tablespoons lemon juice
- 2 tablespoons sweet tomato chutney
- 2 tablespoons single cream
- 300 ml/½ pint mayonnaise
- salt and pepper

1 To make the dressing, heat the oil in a pan and fry the onion until soft. Add the curry powder and cook for *1–2 minutes*. Stir in the stock, lemon juice, chutney and salt and pepper to taste and bring to the boil. Cook for *5 minutes*. Allow to cool.

2 Meanwhile, remove the skin from the cold roast chicken and chop the meat into bite-sized pieces.

3 Strain the curry mixture into a large bowl. Add the cream and mayonnaise and stir to mix. Stir in the chopped chicken.

4 Line individual serving plates with the lettuce leaves and top with the chicken mixture. Sprinkle with toasted almonds.

Serves 4–6

Smoked Chicken and Pear Salad

Preparation time: 20–30 minutes

- ½ smoked chicken, skinned, boned and chopped
- 4 teaspoons soured cream
- mixed salad leaves
- 2 ripe pears, such as Comice
- pinch of paprika
- chives, chopped, to garnish

DRESSING:
- 1 tablespoon cider or white wine vinegar
- 4 tablespoons sunflower or rapeseed oil
- ½ teaspoon Dijon mustard
- salt and pepper

1 Mix together the dressing ingredients in a screw-top jar, shake vigorously and set aside.

2 In a bowl, mix the chopped smoked chicken with the soured cream and set aside.

3 Arrange the salad leaves on a large serving platter or in individual serving dishes. Halve, core and slice the pears. Arrange decoratively on the salad leaves and drizzle the dressing over and around the plate. Add the chicken and soured cream, sprinkle with paprika, garnish with chopped chives and serve immediately.

Serves 4

variation
Smoked Chicken and Avocado Salad

Preparation time: 20–30 minutes

1 Follow the main recipe, substituting 2 ripe avocados for the pears. Peel, halve, stone and slice the avocados and toss the slices in lemon juice to prevent discoloration. Arrange the slices fanned out around the edges of the serving plates.

Warm Chicken, Tarragon and Orange Salad

Preparation time: 20 minutes, plus cooling
Cooking time: 45 minutes–1 hour

- 1.5 kg/3 lb chicken
- 1 onion, thinly sliced
- juice and grated rind of
  1 orange
- 1 tablespoon chopped
  tarragon
- 1 bay leaf
- 1 tablespoon olive oil
- 1 tablespoon white wine
  vinegar
- salt and pepper

TO GARNISH:

- 1 small orange, thinly sliced
- small bunch of mustard and
  cress, chopped
- tarragon sprigs (optional)

1 Put the chicken, sliced onion, orange juice and rind, tarragon and bay leaf in a large saucepan. Pour enough water over the chicken to cover it and sprinkle with salt and pepper to taste. Cover, bring to the boil, and simmer for *45 minutes–1 hour*, or until the chicken is cooked.

2 Lift the chicken out of the saucepan and leave to cool. Discard the bay leaf and onion. Measure the stock. Boil the chicken stock until it has reduced to 300 ml/½ pint. Set aside to cool, then chill in the refrigerator.

3 When the chicken is cold, take the meat off the bones and discard the skin. Cut the meat into bite-sized pieces and place in a bowl.

4 When the stock has chilled, remove and discard the layer of fat from the top, then reheat gently to thin it. Stir in the oil, and add the wine vinegar, and salt and pepper to taste. Pour this dressing over the chicken and toss well.

5 Serve immediately, garnished with orange slices, mustard and cress and tarragon sprigs. The salad may also be served on a bed of lettuce.

Serves 4

Pesto Chicken and Pepper Salad

Preparation time: 20 minutes
Cooking time: 20 minutes

- 1 small cooked chicken
- 1 red pepper
- 1 yellow pepper
- 75 g/3 oz mixed salad leaves
  (such as rocket, frisée,
  young spinach)
- 50 g/2 oz black olives
- 1 quantity Pesto Dressing
- olive oil, to drizzle
- salt and pepper
- basil sprigs, to garnish

1 Skin the chicken and remove all the meat from the carcass. Shred the meat and set aside.

2 Cook the peppers under a preheated hot grill for 15–20 minutes, turning occasionally, until the skin is blistered and blackened all over. Transfer the peppers to a plastic bag and set aside to cool.

3 When the peppers are cool enough to handle, rub off and discard the charred skin. Slice the flesh into thin strips, and discard the seeds and core. Season with salt and pepper.

4 Arrange the salad leaves on a serving dish or individual plates. Pile the peppers on to the salad leaves, with the olives and chicken. Spoon the pesto over the chicken mixture. Serve at once, drizzled with olive oil and garnished with sprigs of basil.

Serves 4

Pesto Dressing

Preparation time: 5 minutes

- 25 g/1 oz basil leaves
- 25 g/1 oz Parmesan cheese,
  grated
- 4 tablespoons white wine
  vinegar
- 1 tablespoon pine nuts
- 1 garlic clove, crushed
- 125 ml/4 oz extra-virgin
  olive oil
- pepper

1 Combine the basil leaves, Parmesan, vinegar, pine nuts and garlic in a food processor or liquidizer. Add pepper to taste. Process for a few seconds.

2 With the motor running, drizzle in the olive oil through the feeder tube until the mixture becomes thick and smooth. Pour into a bowl or jug and use as required.

3 This dressing can also be made using a mortar and pestle. Pound together the basil, pine nuts and garlic to form a thick paste. Add the Parmesan, vinegar, pepper and oil and stir vigorously to mix.

Quick and Easy

Scrumptious meals that will look and taste as though they took hours, rather than minutes, to prepare and cook. With many subtle yet distinctive flavours, not only are they quick and easy to make, they are also attractive and appetizing. A selection of exciting dishes that will bring you a multitude of flavours with a minimum of fuss.

Chicken Pilau

Preparation time: 10 minutes, plus marinating
Cooking time: 40 minutes

- 2 kg/4 lb chicken, cut into pieces
- 3 tablespoons groundnut oil
- 15 g/½ oz butter
- 1 onion, finely chopped
- 2 garlic cloves, crushed
- 1 red pepper, cored, deseeded and chopped
- 1 red chilli, deseeded and finely chopped
- 375 g/12 oz long-grain rice
- 2 tomatoes, skinned and chopped
- 900 ml/1½ pints Chicken Stock (see page 8)
- few saffron threads (optional)
- 1 thyme sprig

SEASONING:
- 1 teaspoon dried mixed herbs
- 2 allspice berries (optional)
- 1 garlic clove, peeled
- salt and pepper

TO GARNISH:
- 50 g/2 oz roasted peanuts
- chopped red chilli
- chopped thyme

1 Put the seasoning ingredients in a mortar and pound well with a pestle until the garlic and allspice berries (if using) are crushed and blended with the salt, pepper and herbs. Rub this mixture all over the chicken pieces and leave to marinate in a cool place or in the refrigerator for several hours (or overnight if wished).

2 Heat the oil and butter in a large, deep frying pan and add the seasoned chicken pieces. Fry over moderate heat, turning several times, until they are golden brown all over. Remove from the pan and keep warm.

3 Add the onion, garlic, red pepper and chilli to the pan, and fry over gentle heat until softened but not browned. Add the rice to the pan and turn in the oil until all the grains are glistening. Stir in the tomatoes, chicken stock, saffron threads (if using) and thyme.

4 Return the chicken pieces to the pan, cover and simmer for about *20 minutes*, or until the rice is tender and has absorbed all the liquid, and the chicken is cooked. Keep checking the pan and stirring the rice to prevent it sticking. Add more liquid if necessary. Serve hot sprinkled with peanuts, chilli and chopped thyme.

Serves 6

Chicken and Smoked Ham Gumbo

Gumbo is a soupy stew from Louisiana, usually made with seafood, such as prawns, crab and scallops. Here it is made with chicken and smoked ham, which is equally delicious. As a variation, you can substitute 375 g/12 oz peeled prawns or 8 scallops for the ham and cook them for just a few minutes.

Preparation time: 20 minutes
Cooking time: about 1 hour

- 5 tablespoons rapeseed or olive oil
- 40 g/1½ oz plain flour
- 1 large onion, finely chopped
- 1 red pepper, cored, deseeded and finely chopped
- 2 garlic cloves, finely chopped
- 1.2 litres/2 pints Chicken Stock (see page 8)
- 400 g/13 oz can chopped tomatoes
- 2 tablespoons chopped parsley
- 1 tablespoon chopped thyme
- ¼ teaspoon cayenne pepper
- 750 g/1½ lb skinless and boneless chicken thighs, cut into bite-sized pieces
- 250 g/8 oz okra, thinly sliced
- 250 g/8 oz smoked ham in one piece, cut into bite-sized pieces
- salt and pepper
- deep-fried thyme and parsley sprigs, to garnish (optional)

1 Heat the oil in a large flameproof casserole, sprinkle in the flour and stir well to form a roux. Cook the roux, stirring constantly, over a gentle heat for about *2 minutes* until it is a rich, nutty brown in colour.

2 Add the onion, red pepper and garlic and fry, stirring frequently, for about *5 minutes* until softened.

3 Gradually stir in the stock, then add the tomatoes, herbs, cayenne and salt and pepper to taste. Increase the heat and bring to the boil, stirring.

4 Lower the heat and add the chicken and okra. Cover the casserole and simmer over a gentle heat, stirring occasionally, for *40 minutes* or until the chicken is tender when pierced with a skewer or fork. Add the smoked ham for the last *10 minutes* of the cooking time.

5 Adjust the seasoning to taste and serve hot, garnished with deep-fried sprigs of thyme and parsley, if liked.

Serves 6

Minced Chicken with Basil

Preparation time: 3 minutes
Cooking time: 6 minutes

- 5 small green chillies
- 2 garlic cloves
- 2 tablespoons oil
- 125 g/4 oz minced chicken
- 1 shallot, chopped
- 25 g/1 oz bamboo shoots
- 25 g/1 oz red pepper cored, deseeded and chopped
- 15 g/½ oz carrot, diced
- 1 teaspoon palm sugar or light muscovado sugar
- 3 tablespoons Thai fish sauce (*nam pla*) or light soy sauce
- 3 tablespoons Chicken Stock (see page 8)
- 15 g/½ oz basil leaves, finely chopped
- 1 quantity Crispy Garlic, Shallots and Basil, to garnish

1 Put the chillies and garlic into a mortar and pound with a pestle until well broken down.

2 Heat the oil in a wok, add the chillies and garlic and stir-fry for *30 seconds*. Add the remaining ingredients and cook, stirring, for *4 minutes* over a moderate heat. Turn the heat up high and continue stirring vigorously for *30 seconds*.

3 Turn on to a dish and serve with rice, garnished with Crispy Garlic, Shallots and Basil.

Serves 2 as a main course or 4 as a starter

Crispy Garlic, Shallots and Basil

Preparation time: 5 minutes
Cooking time: about 5–6 minutes

- 25 g/1 oz garlic, finely chopped
- 25 g/1 oz shallots, finely chopped
- 25 g/1 oz basil leaves
- 1 small red chilli, finely sliced
- groundnut oil, for deep-frying

1 Heat the oil in a wok. When hot, add the garlic and stir for about *40 seconds.*

2 Remove with a slotted spoon, draining as much oil as possible back into the wok, then spread out to dry on absorbent kitchen paper. Repeat the process with the shallots allowing *1½–2 minutes* frying time. Then add the basil leaves and chilli to the oil and fry for about *1 minute*. Remove with a slotted spoon and drain as before.

Cranberry Chicken Stir-fry with Ginger

Preparation time: 20 minutes
Cooking time: 10 minutes

- 2 tablespoons vegetable oil
- 2 shallots, finely chopped
- 2.5 cm/1 inch piece of fresh root ginger, peeled and thinly sliced into matchsticks
- 2 garlic cloves, crushed
- 4 skinless, boneless chicken breasts, finely sliced
- 2 tablespoons hoisin sauce or dark soy sauce
- 2 tablespoons oyster sauce (optional)

- 1 tablespoon light soy sauce
- 25 g/1 oz dried cranberries
- 4 spring onions, diagonally sliced
- 175 g/6 oz bean sprouts, or sliced green or red pepper or carrot strips

TO GARNISH:
- handful of basil leaves
- 1 large red chilli, deseeded and finely sliced
- vegetable oil, for deep-frying

1 Heat the oil in a wok and stir-fry the shallots, ginger and garlic for *30 seconds*. Add the chicken and stir-fry for *2 minutes* or until golden brown.

2 Add the hoisin, oyster, and soy sauces and the cranberries and stir-fry for a further *2 minutes*. Check that the chicken is cooked all the way through, then add the onions and bean sprouts or other vegetables, if using, and toss together for *3–4 minutes*.

3 To make the garnish, heat 1 cm/½ inch oil in a small saucepan and deep-fry the basil leaves and red chilli in two batches for *10–30 seconds* until crisp. Remove with a slotted spoon and drain on kitchen paper.

Serves 4

Stir-fried Chicken with Cashew Nuts and Baby Corn

Preparation time: 10 minutes
Cooking time: about 7 minutes

- 3 tablespoons oil
- 125 g/4 oz chicken, skinned and cut into bite-sized pieces
- ¼ onion, sliced
- 50 g/2 oz baby corn, obliquely sliced
- 50 g/2 oz cashew nuts
- 125 ml/4 fl oz light soy sauce
- 4 tablespoons Chicken Stock (see page 8)
- 4 teaspoons palm sugar or light muscovado sugar
- 15 g/½ oz spring onion, obliquely sliced
- black pepper
- 1 large red chilli, obliquely sliced, to garnish

1 Heat the oil in a wok, add the chicken, onion, baby corn and cashew nuts. Stir-fry over a high heat for *3 minutes*.

2 Reduce the heat and stir in the soy sauce. Then add the stock, sugar and spring onion and season with black pepper. Raise the heat and stir-fry for another *2 minutes*.

3 Turn on to a serving dish or into 2 individual bowls, sprinkle with sliced chilli and serve.

Serves 2

Stir-fried Chicken with Pineapple

Preparation time: 10 minutes
Cooking time: 12–14 minutes

- 50 g/2 oz tempura flour or self-raising flour
- 75 ml/3 fl oz water
- 125 g/4 oz chicken, skinned and cut into bite-sized pieces
- 1 tablespoon oil
- 150 g/5 oz fresh pineapple, cut into chunks
- 1 tomato, cut into 8 pieces
- 1 tablespoon tomato purée

- 1 tablespoon palm sugar or light muscovado sugar
- 50 g/2 oz cashew nuts
- 1½ tablespoons light soy sauce
- oil, for deep-frying

TO GARNISH:

- alfalfa or bean sprouts
- coriander sprigs
- ½ lime

1 Heat the oil for deep-frying in a wok or large frying pan and, while it is heating, mix the flour and water together thoroughly to make a coating batter.

2 When the oil is hot enough, coat half the chicken pieces in the batter and deep-fry them until they are golden brown. Remove them from the oil and drain on kitchen paper. Repeat with the remaining chicken.

3 Pour off the oil, wipe the wok clean with absorbent kitchen paper then heat the 1 tablespoon of oil. Add the pineapple, tomato, tomato purée, sugar and cashews and stir-fry for *2 minutes*. Add the soy sauce and stir.

4 Serve the batter-coated chicken on the tomato and pineapple mixture, garnished with alfalfa or bean sprouts, coriander sprigs and lime.

Serves 4

Classic Ingredients

Chicken is so popular because there are many good accompanying ingredients and flavourings to complement it. Traditionally it has been flavoured with herbs, marinated, or served with vegetables, simply but deliciously.

Horseradish

Wholegrain mustard

Pine nuts

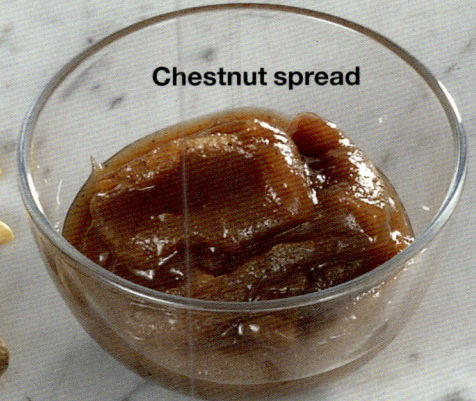

Chestnut spread

Nutmeg

Juniper berries

Dried cranberries

Whole cloves

Horseradish is cultivated mainly for its root, which is used as a condiment. Its sharp, hot flavour is generally softened by adding milk and breadcrumbs.

Wholegrain mustard is a mixture of crushed and uncrushed mustard seeds, served as a condiment or added to sauces. It has a distinctive hot flavour.

Pine nuts are the seeds of the stone pine tree which are extracted from between the scales of the pine cones. They have a nutty flavour which goes well with chicken.

Nutmeg is the seed of the nutmeg tree. It is grated and used as a spice in both sweet and savoury dishes. Use as a flavouring in stuffings for chicken.

Chestnut spread is puréed cooked chestnuts and is highly nutritious. It is delicious in stuffings and soups.

Juniper Berries are used in cooking and also in wines and spirits. Their strong flavour is indispensible when making marinades for poultry and game dishes.

Dried cranberries have a much sweeter and more intense flavour than fresh cranberries. They can be used in stuffings and sauces to accompany chicken dishes.

Bouquet garni

Fennel

Sage

Coriander

Yellow onion

Tarragon

Rosemary

Celery

Whole cloves are the sundried flower buds of the clove tree. They are used as a spice in many chicken dishes. Traditionally they have been used as a meat preservative.
Bouquet garni is a small bundle of aromatic herbs, bound together, and used to flavour stocks and sauces.

Fennel has a slight aniseed flavour. The bulb can be roasted, braised or eaten raw in salads. Its feathery leaves make an attractive garnish.
Sage is a slightly bitter herb used in soups or with white meat. Sage and onion stuffing is the traditional partner to roast chicken.

Yellow onion is a mild-flavoured vegetable used in soups, stews and often cooked with chicken.
Celery stems, leaves, seeds and roots can all be eaten and are used in many dishes.
Tarragon is a particularly delicious flavouring for chicken. It also makes an

attractive garnish.
Coriander seeds are ground or used whole as flavourings; the leaves are similar in shape to parsley and are also used as a flavouring.
Rosemary has evergreen leaves which are used fresh or dried to flavour savoury dishes.

Chilli Chicken with Pine Nuts

Preparation time: 30 minutes
Cooking time: 15 minutes

- 4 boneless chicken breasts
- 4 tablespoons sunflower oil
- 1 red pepper, cored, deseeded and cut into strips
- 1 green pepper, cored, deseeded and cut into strips
- 1 red chilli, deseeded and finely chopped
- 1 green chilli, deseeded and finely chopped, plus extra to garnish
- 50 g/2 oz pine nuts
- 1 garlic clove, finely chopped
- 4 tablespoons dry white wine
- 2 tablespoons lemon juice
- 3 tablespoons oyster sauce or dark soy sauce
- 2 teaspoons caster sugar
- 1 teaspoon chilli sauce
- 4 tablespoons light soy sauce
- 1 tablespoon cornflour
- salt and pepper
- ½ lime, to serve

TO GARNISH:
- 2 spring onions, sliced
- flat leaf parsley

1 Cut the chicken into 1 x 5 cm/½ x 2 inch strips. Season with salt and pepper. Heat 2 tablespoons of the oil in a wok or large frying pan, add the chicken strips and cook, stirring constantly, for *5 minutes*, or until tender. Remove the chicken and reserve.

2 Heat the remaining oil in the wok or frying pan and stir-fry the red and green pepper strips for *2 minutes*, until just cooked. Lift out and reserve.

3 Add the chillies, pine nuts and garlic to the pan and stir-fry for *1 minute*. Drain and discard any excess fat, then add the white wine, lemon juice, oyster sauce, caster sugar and chilli sauce. Cook, stirring frequently, for *1 minute*.

4 Blend together the soy sauce and cornflour, add to the chilli mixture and bring to the boil. Return the chicken and pepper to the wok or frying pan, then cover and cook over a moderate heat until warmed through. Serve at once with the lime, garnished with spring onions, flat leaf parsley and green chilli.

Serves 4

Sauté of Chicken with Garlic, Lemon and Herbs

Preparation time: 10 minutes
Cooking time: 35–45 minutes

- 4 tablespoons extra virgin olive oil
- 3 garlic cloves, chopped
- 4 chicken portions
- finely grated rind and juice of 1 lemon
- 1 tablespoon chopped flat leaf parsley
- 2 teaspoons chopped tarragon
- salt and pepper

TO GARNISH:
- ½ lemon
- tarragon sprigs
- flat leaf parsley sprigs

1 Heat the oil in a large frying pan, add the garlic and sauté until lightly coloured but not browned.

2 Add the chicken in a single layer, season to taste and sauté, turning frequently, for *15–20 minutes* until the skin is crisp and golden brown.

3 Lower the heat, cover the pan and continue cooking for *15–20 minutes* until the juices run clear when the thickest part is pierced with a skewer or fork.

4 Remove the chicken from the pan with a slotted spoon and place on a warmed serving platter.

5 Add the lemon rind and juice to the pan and stir well until sizzling to dislodge any sediment in the bottom of the pan.

6 Remove from the heat and add the herbs and salt and pepper to taste. Stir well to mix, then pour over the chicken. Serve hot, garnished with lemon, tarragon and flat leaf parsley. A crisp green or mixed salad and French fries would make suitable accompaniments.

Serves 4

Chicken with Cream Cheese, Garlic and Herbs

Preparation time: 15 minutes
Cooking time: 20 minutes
Oven temperature: 220°C (425°F), Gas Mark 7

- 4 boneless chicken breasts
- 125 g/4 oz cream cheese or
  low-fat soft cheese
- 3 tablespoons finely chopped
  mixed herbs (such as
  tarragon, dill, parsley, chervil)
- 1–2 garlic cloves, crushed

- 15 g/½ oz butter
- salt and pepper

TO GARNISH:
- olive oil with chopped herbs
- ½ lemon with twisted rind
- rosemary sprigs

1 Insert your fingers between the skin and the flesh of each chicken breast to make a pocket.

2 Put the cheese in a bowl with the herbs, garlic and salt and pepper to taste. Beat well to mix. Push the cheese mixture into the pockets in the chicken breasts, dividing it equally between them. Smooth the skin over the cheese to make it as compact as possible.

3 Melt the butter in a small saucepan, then use to brush a baking dish. Arrange the chicken breasts in a single layer in the dish, then brush with the remaining butter and season with salt and pepper to taste.

4 Cook in a preheated oven, 220°C (425°F), Gas Mark 7, for *20 minutes* or until the chicken is cooked through and tender when pierced with a skewer or fork.

5 Serve hot, cut diagonally into slices if liked, drizzled with olive oil and fresh chopped herbs and garnished with lemon and rosemary sprigs. A green salad would make a good accompaniment.

Serves 4

Easy Chicken Kievs

Preparation time: 20 minutes, plus freezing
Cooking time: 30–40 minutes
Oven temperature: 190°C (375°F), Gas Mark 5

- **4 boneless, skinless chicken breasts**
- **2 garlic cloves, crushed**
- **grated rind of 1 lemon**
- **125 g/4 oz butter**
- **1 tablespoon chopped parsley**
- **25 g/1 oz plain flour**
- **1 egg, lightly beaten**
- **125 g/4 oz fresh white breadcrumbs**
- **salt and pepper**

TO GARNISH:
- **½ lemon**
- **flat leaf parsley**

1 Beat the chicken breasts flat with a rolling pin or the base of a pan. Mix together the garlic, lemon rind, butter, parsley and salt and pepper to form a paste. Spread the butter mixture evenly over each chicken breast and carefully roll up. Secure with string or clingfilm.

2 Freeze for *15 minutes*, or until the butter is firm. Coat the chicken in the flour, dip in the beaten egg and coat in the breadcrumbs, pressing firmly to make sure they stick. Return to the freezer for a further *15 minutes*.

3 Bake the chicken in a preheated hot oven, 190°C (375°F), Gas Mark 5, for *30–40 minutes* or until the outside is golden and crisp and the chicken is cooked right through.

4 Serve garnished with lemon and flat leaf parsley. Boiled vegetables make a good accompaniment.

Serves 4

Chicken and Prawn Kebabs

Preparation time: 15 minutes, plus marinating
Cooking time: about 20 minutes

- 750 g/1½ lb skinless, boneless chicken breast, cut into 2.5 cm/1 inch cubes
- 20 cooked Mediterranean or large prawns, defrosted if frozen
- 1 small yellow or red pepper, cored, deseeded and cut into 2.5 cm/1 inch squares
- 1 small green pepper, cored, deseeded and cut into 2.5 cm/1 inch squares
- 1 quantity Herb Marinade
- potato salad, to serve

TO GARNISH:
- lime wedges
- marjoram seeds (optional)

1 Thread the chicken, prawns and peppers alternately on to presoaked bamboo or oiled metal skewers.

2 Place the skewers in a shallow dish and pour over the marinade. Turn the skewers to coat with the marinade. Cover and leave to marinate for *2 hours* in a cool place, turning occasionally.

3 Remove the kebabs from the marinade, reserving the marinade. Cook the kebabs under a preheated moderate hot grill or on a barbecue for about *20 minutes*, turning and basting frequently with the reserved marinade.

4 Serve with potato salad, garnished with a lime wedge and marjoram seeds, if using, and any remaining herb marinade.

Serves 6–8

Herb Marinade

Follow the recipe or choose any other fresh herbs you like such as chives, oregano, rosemary and sage for this marinade.

Preparation time: 5 minutes

- 4 tablespoons sunflower oil
- 2 tablespoons lemon juice
- 1 teaspoon chopped marjoram
- 1 teaspoon chopped thyme
- 2 tablespoons chopped parsley
- 1 garlic clove, crushed
- 1 onion, finely chopped
- salt and pepper

1 Mix together all the ingredients in a bowl with salt and pepper to taste, or place in a screw-top jar and shake well.

Chicken and Sweet Pepper Kebabs

Cut the chicken, onion and red pepper into chunks of roughly the same size. This gives the kebabs a neat appearance and helps ensure even cooking.

Preparation time: 15 minutes, plus marinating
Cooking time: 20 minutes

- 150 ml/¼ pint natural yogurt
- 2 tablespoons extra virgin olive oil
- 2 garlic cloves, crushed
- 2 tablespoons chopped fresh coriander
- 2 tablespoons ground cumin
- 8 skinless, boneless chicken thighs, cut into large chunks
- 1 onion, cut into chunks
- 1 red pepper, cored, deseeded and cut into chunks
- 1 green pepper, cored, deseeded and cut into chunks
- salt and pepper

TO SERVE:
- mixed salad leaves
- lime wedges

1 Mix together the yogurt, oil, garlic, coriander and cumin in a shallow dish with salt and pepper to taste. Add the pieces of chicken and stir well to mix. Cover and marinate at room temperature for *30 minutes–1 hour*.

2 Thread the pieces of chicken on to presoaked bamboo or oiled metal skewers, alternating them with pieces of onion and red and green pepper.

3 Cook the kebabs under a preheated hot grill, turning frequently, for *20 minutes* or until the chicken is tender when pierced with a skewer or fork. Serve hot, on a bed of mixed salad leaves, garnished with lime wedges.

Serves 4

Livers Oporto

Preparation time: 10 minutes
Cooking time: 10 minutes

- 25 g/1 oz butter
- 1 tablespoon oil
- 500 g/1 lb chicken livers, trimmed and halved
- 3 celery sticks, sliced

- 4 tablespoons port
- 5 tablespoons soured cream
- salt and pepper
- celery leaves, to garnish

1 Heat the butter and oil in a large frying pan, add the livers and celery and sauté for *3–4 minutes*, until the livers are golden outside but still pink inside. When cooked, remove the livers from the pan and keep warm.

2 To make the sauce, add the port to the pan and simmer for a few minutes, until slightly reduced. Add the soured cream, tilting the pan to mix, and continue cooking gently until a smooth sauce forms. Season with salt and pepper to taste.

3 Serve the livers on top of the sauce, garnished with celery leaves. Pasta tossed in garlic-flavoured butter would make a good accompaniment.

Serves 4

variation
Chicken Oporto

Preparation time: 10 minutes
Cooking time: 15 minutes

- 25 g/1 oz butter
- 1 tablespoon oil
- 1 onion, sliced
- 4 skinless, boneless chicken breasts

- 3 celery sticks, sliced
- 4 tablespoons port
- 5 tablespoons soured cream
- salt and pepper
- celery leaves, to garnish

1 Heat the butter and oil in a large frying pan, add the onion and fry gently for 5 minutes, until soft but not brown.

2 Slice the chicken breasts into 1 x 5 cm/½ x 2 inch pieces. Add the chicken and celery to the pan and sauté for *5–7 minutes*, or until the chicken is cooked right through. Remove the chicken from the pan and keep warm.

3 Follow steps 2 and 3 of the main recipe to finish the dish.

Serves 4

International Chicken

From the mystical spices of the Far East and the influences of the Orient, to the distinguished culinary traditions of the Europeans, these recipes bring the flavours of the world to your fingertips. Delicious combinations of chicken with seafood, coconut, fruit, herbs and spices create a wide array of flavours, giving your cooking an enticing new dimension.

Chicken and Mango Spring Rolls with Sweet Chilli Dipping Sauce

Preparation time: 20 minutes, plus cooling
Cooking time: 30 minutes

- 1 teaspoon grated fresh root ginger
- 4 tablespoons dark soy sauce
- 4 skinless, boneless chicken breasts
- 8 spring roll wrappers
- 1 firm mango, peeled and thinly sliced
- 1 small bunch of coriander, chopped
- 1 dessertspoon flour and 3 dessertspoons water, mixed to a paste
- vegetable oil, for deep-frying

SWEET CHILLI DIPPING SAUCE:
- 1 tablespoon olive oil
- 2 shallots, finely chopped

- 2 garlic cloves, crushed
- 250 g/8 oz canned chopped tomatoes
- 3 tablespoons bottled sweet chilli sauce
- 50 g/2 oz caster sugar
- 3 tablespoons white wine vinegar
- 3 tablespoons water
- 1 red chilli, deseeded and finely chopped
- 1 carrot, peeled and shredded

TO SERVE:
- 2 tablespoons sunflower oil
- 2 tablespoons lime juice
- mixed salad leaves

1 Mix the ginger and soy sauce together. Baste the chicken breasts with the mixture, then bake in a preheated oven, 190°C (375°F), Gas Mark 5, for *15–20 minutes*. When cooked through, leave to cool, then slice as finely as possible.

2 Meanwhile, make the sweet chilli dipping sauce. Heat the oil in a frying pan and fry the shallots and garlic for a few minutes to soften, then add the tomatoes and simmer until the liquid has reduced by half. Remove from the heat and allow to cool. Then strain through a sieve and stir in the bottled sweet chilli sauce.

3 Put the sugar, vinegar, water and chilli in a small saucepan and heat gently to dissolve the sugar, then stir in the shredded carrot. Allow to cool, then stir into the tomato mixture.

4 Place the spring roll wrappers on a clean work surface. Divide the chicken, mango slices and coriander between the wrappers leaving a 2½ cm/1 inch border around the edge of each wrapper. Brush the border with the flour and water paste, then fold in the two edges, seal again with paste then tightly roll the wrapper to enclose the filling. Repeat the process until you have 8 filled rolls.

5 Heat the oil for deep-frying, then add the spring rolls, 2 at a time, and cook until golden brown. Drain on kitchen paper.

6 To serve, combine the oil and lime juice. Put the salad leaves in a bowl and toss with the oil and lime juice dressing. Arrange the leaves on a serving plate with the hot spring rolls and the sweet chilli sauce on the side.

Serves 4

Malaysian Chicken, Noodle and Prawn Stew

The combination of poultry and seafood is very popular in the Far East, and you will find it absolutely delicious.

Preparation time: 20 minutes
Cooking time: 30 minutes

- 2 tablespoons oil
- 4–6 spring onions, shredded
- 5 cm/2 inch piece of fresh root ginger, peeled and cut into very thin matchsticks
- 2 garlic cloves, crushed
- 375 g/12 oz skinless chicken breast, cut diagonally into thin strips
- 2 tablespoons rice wine or dry sherry
- 2 tablespoons soy sauce
- 1 teaspoon turmeric
- 1 teaspoon chilli powder
- 1.8 litres/3 pints Chicken Stock (see page 8)
- 2 tablespoons Thai fish sauce (*nam pla*) or light soy sauce
- 125 g/4 oz creamed coconut, roughly chopped
- 2 carrots, cut into very thin matchsticks
- 250 g/8 oz French beans, cut diagonally into 5 cm/2 inch lengths
- 125 g/4 oz Chinese egg noodles
- 125 g/4 oz bean sprouts
- 8–12 large raw prawns in their shells
- salt and pepper

1 Heat the oil in a large flameproof casserole and stir-fry the spring onions, ginger and garlic for about *5 minutes* until softened but not coloured.

2 Add the chicken and stir-fry until it changes colour, then stir in the rice wine or sherry, soy sauce, turmeric, chilli powder and salt and pepper to taste.

3 Gradually add the stock and fish sauce, stirring constantly to mix with the chicken and flavouring ingredients. Add the creamed coconut and simmer, stirring constantly, for about *5 minutes* until the coconut has dissolved. Cover and simmer gently for about *10 minutes* until the chicken is just tender.

4 Add the carrots and French beans, cover and simmer for a further *5 minutes*. Add the noodles, bean sprouts and prawns, cover and remove from the heat. Leave to stand for *5 minutes* until the noodles are soft and the prawns pink.

5 Remove the prawns from the casserole and pull off their shells with your fingers. Slice the prawns horizontally in half, then return to the casserole and stir well to mix. Adjust the seasoning to taste and serve hot, in warmed bowls.

Serves 6–8

Chicken Satay

Garam masala is readily available but if you want to make your own, mix together 2 teaspoons of ground coriander seeds, 1 teaspoon of ground cumin seeds, 1 teaspoon of ground turmeric, ¼ teaspoon of ground cinnamon, ¼ teaspoon of ground cloves and a pinch of ground nutmeg. Store any left over in an airtight container and use within a few weeks.

Preparation time: 30 minutes, plus marinating
Cooking time: 10 minutes

- 500 g/1 lb boneless, skinless chicken breast
- 1 small onion, chopped
- 2 cm/¾ inch piece of fresh root ginger, peeled and sliced
- 1 large garlic clove, sliced
- 1 tablespoon lemon juice
- 2 teaspoons garam masala
- ¼ teaspoon salt
- 1 teaspoon granulated sugar
- 1 tablespoon light soy sauce
- lime wedges, to garnish
- rocket, to serve (optional)

SATAY SAUCE:
- 6 tablespoons desiccated coconut
- 250 ml/8 fl oz boiling water
- 4 tablespoons peanut butter
- 1 tablespoon oil
- 2 large garlic cloves, crushed
- ¼–½ teaspoon chilli powder
- 1 tablespoon dark soy sauce

1 Cut the chicken into 1 cm/½ inch cubes. Place in a mixing bowl and set aside.

2 Put the onion, ginger and garlic in a food processor or blender. Add the lemon juice and blend to a purée. Add to the chicken cubes, with the garam masala, salt, sugar and soy sauce. Mix well, cover and leave to marinate for *1 hour*, stirring from time to time.

3 Meanwhile, prepare the satay sauce. Place the coconut in a bowl. Pour over the boiling water and leave for *30 minutes*. Strain through a sieve set over a bowl, pressing the coconut against the sides of the sieve to extract as much liquid (coconut milk) as possible. Discard the coconut. Stir the peanut butter into the coconut milk. Set aside.

4 In a small saucepan, heat the oil over a low heat. Add the garlic and cook until soft but not brown. Add the chilli powder and cook for a few seconds. Stir in the peanut butter and coconut milk mixture with the soy sauce and continue to stir over a low heat until thickened and hot. Keep warm.

5 Thread the chicken cubes on to presoaked wooden or oiled metal skewers. Cook under a preheated hot grill for *2 minutes* on each side. Serve with the hot satay sauce piped on to plates, and garnish with lime wedges. Serve with a bowl of rocket, if liked.

Serves 4

Chinese Chicken with Black Beans

Preparation time: 15 minutes, plus soaking and marinating
Cooking time: 1¾ hours

- 2 tablespoons salted black beans
- 1.5 kg/3 lb roasting chicken
- 1 tablespoon vegetable oil
- 1 teaspoon dark sesame oil
- 6 spring onions, diagonally sliced
- 1–2 red chillies, deseeded and thinly sliced
- 3 tablespoons dry sherry
- 1 teaspoon sugar
- 1 tablespoon cornflour, mixed with 3 tablespoons water

MARINADE:
- 25 g/1 oz fresh root ginger, peeled and coarsely grated
- 1–2 tablespoons soy sauce
- pepper

TO GARNISH:
- spring onion fans
- red pepper strips

1 Soak the salted black beans in cold water for *20 minutes*; drain well and set aside.

2 Mix the marinade ingredients together, with pepper to taste, and use to coat the chicken inside and out. Put the chicken in a roasting bag, tie loosely and place in a roasting tin. Leave for *4–6 hours*, then make several holes in the bag, following the manufacturer's instructions.

3 Cook in a preheated oven, 180°C (350°F), Gas Mark 4, for *1¼ hours*. Remove the chicken from the bag, reserving the juices, and place in the roasting tin. Increase the oven temperature to 200°C (400°F), Gas Mark 6 and cook for a further *25–30 minutes*, until the juices run clear.

4 Meanwhile, heat the vegetable and sesame oils in a pan, add the spring onions and stir-fry over high heat for *30 seconds*. Add the chillies and black beans and cook for *2 minutes*. Skim off as much fat as possible from the contents of the roasting bag. Add the remaining liquid to the pan with the sherry and sugar. Stir in the blended cornflour and cook until clear and syrupy.

5 Carve the chicken and arrange on a warmed serving dish. Pour over the sauce. Garnish with spring onion fans and red pepper strips.

Serves 4

Spring Onion Fans

Trim the tops off the spring onions and remove the root base. Carefully slit both ends, leaving the middle part intact. Leave in a bowl of iced water until the spring onions have opened up into fans.

Szechuan Fried Chicken

Preparation time: 10–15 minutes, plus soaking
Cooking time: 10–15 minutes

- 4 boneless, skinless chicken breasts, cut into bite-sized strips
- 1 teaspoon salt
- 1 tablespoon cornflour
- 250 g/8 oz bamboo shoots, cut into large dice
- 3 tablespoons hoisin sauce or dark soy sauce
- 4 tablespoons yellow bean sauce
- 1 teaspoon light soy sauce
- 2 teaspoons white wine vinegar
- 4 tablespoons oil
- 6 garlic cloves, sliced
- ½ teaspoon Szechuan or mixed peppercorns, crushed
- 2 tablespoons sherry

TO GARNISH:

- sesame seeds
- coriander sprigs
- ½ lime

1 Place the chicken pieces in a bowl, add the salt and pour over cold water to cover. Leave to soak for *20 minutes*. Drain the chicken, pat dry with kitchen paper and toss in the cornflour until thoroughly coated.

2 In a separate bowl, mix the bamboo shoots with the hoisin, yellow bean and soy sauces and vinegar.

3 Heat a wok. Add the oil and when hot, stir-fry the chicken, garlic and pepper for *2–3 minutes*. Add the bamboo shoot mixture, stir well and cook for *1 minute* further. Add the sherry, stir and simmer until the sauce thickens. Transfer to a warmed serving platter and serve immediately garnished with sesame seeds, coriander sprigs and lime.

Serves 4

Green Curry Chicken

Preparation time: 5–7 minutes
Cooking time: 13–15 minutes

- 1 tablespoon oil
- 1½ tablespoons Green Curry Paste
- 4 tablespoons coconut milk
- 125 g/4 oz chicken breast, cut into bite-sized pieces
- 2 lime leaves, torn, or 2 strips lime rind
- ½ lemon grass stalk, cut in fine, oblique slices (optional)
- 50 g/2 oz bamboo shoots
- 3 small green aubergines, or 1 purple aubergine, chopped
- 50 g/2 oz courgettes, cut in oblique chunks
- 1 large red chilli, obliquely sliced
- 6 tablespoons Chicken Stock (see page 8)
- 1 tablespoon palm sugar or light muscovado sugar
- 3 tablespoons Thai fish sauce (*nam pla*) or light soy sauce
- sweet basil sprigs, to garnish

1 Heat the oil in a wok and stir in the curry paste. Cook for *30 seconds*, then add the coconut milk and cook, stirring, for *1 minute*.

2 Add the chicken, bring up to a simmer and add all the remaining ingredients. Simmer for 10 minutes, stirring occasionally.

3 Transfer the curry to a warmed serving bowl, garnish with basil sprigs and serve.

Serves 2

Green Curry Paste

Preparation time: 15 minutes

- 7 small green chillies
- 2 garlic cloves, halved
- 1 lemon grass stalk, finely chopped (optional)
- 1 lime leaf, torn (optional)
- 1 shallot, chopped
- 25 g/1 oz coriander leaves and stalks
- 1 cm/½ inch piece of fresh root ginger, peeled and chopped
- 1 teaspoon coriander seeds
- ½ teaspoon black peppercorns
- ½ teaspoon grated lime rind
- ¼ teaspoon salt
- 1 tablespoon groundnut oil

1 Put all the ingredients in a food processor or blender and blend to a thick paste.

2 Alternatively, put the chillies into a mortar and crush them with a pestle, then add the garlic and crush it into the chillies, and so on with all the other ingredients, finally stirring in the oil with a spoon.

3 Transfer any leftover paste to an airtight container and store in the refrigerator for up to *3 weeks*.

Chicken Jalfrezi

Preparation time: 10 minutes
Cooking time: 25 minutes

- 6 tablespoons clarified butter or ghee
- 1 teaspoon white cumin seeds
- 1 teaspoon black mustard seeds
- 2–6 garlic cloves, finely chopped
- 5 cm/2 inch piece of fresh root ginger, finely sliced
- 1 large onion, thinly sliced
- 750 g/1½ lb boneless, skinless chicken breast, diced
- 1 tablespoon Mild Curry Paste
- ½ red pepper, cored, deseeded and chopped
- ½ green pepper, cored, deseeded and chopped
- 2 tomatoes, skinned and chopped
- 1 tablespoon chopped coriander leaves
- 1–2 tablespoons water
- coriander sprigs, to garnish

1 Heat the butter or ghee in a large frying pan or wok and stir-fry the cumin and mustard seeds for *1 minute*. Add the garlic and stir-fry for *1 minute* more. Add the ginger and stir-fry for *2 minutes*. Add the sliced onion and stir-fry for about *5 minutes* until golden.

2 Combine the chicken pieces with the spice mixture in the pan and stir-fry for *5 minutes*.

3 Add the curry paste, red and green peppers, tomatoes, coriander and water and stir-fry for around *10 minutes* more. Serve immediately with rice, garnished with coriander sprigs.

Serves 4

Mild Curry Paste

Preparation time: 5 minutes
Cooking time: 15 minutes

- 125 g/4 oz mild curry powder
- 125 ml/4 fl oz vinegar
- 125 ml/4 fl oz vegetable oil

1 Mix the curry powder with the vinegar and enough water to make a paste which is not too runny. Heat the oil in a large frying pan or wok. Add the paste: it will splutter at first but soon settle down. Stir-fry for *15 minutes* or so until the water has completely evaporated to leave a creamy paste. The oil will rise to the surface when the paste is set aside. This means it is fully cooked. Transfer the cooled paste to a warm sterilized bottle. Heat a little more oil and pour it on top of the paste to ensure no mould develops. Cover the bottle tightly with a lid. It will keep indefinitely providing all the water has evaporated. Use as required.

Coconut Grilled Chicken

Preparation time: 6 minutes, plus marinating
Cooking time: 15 minutes

- 2–3 boneless chicken
  breasts

MARINADE:

- 400 ml/13 fl oz can coconut
  milk
- 4 garlic cloves
- 4 small green or red chillies
- 2.5 cm/1 inch piece fresh
  root ginger, peeled and
  sliced
- grated rind and juice of
  1 lime

- 2 tablespoons palm sugar or
  light muscovado sugar
- 3 tablespoons light soy
  sauce
- 1 tablespoon Thai fish sauce
  (*nam pla*) (optional)
- 25 g/1 oz coriander leaves
  and stalks

TO GARNISH:

- 1 red chilli, finely diced
- spring onion slivers

1 To make the marinade, blend together all the ingredients.

2 Make 3 oblique cuts on each side of the chicken breasts, place them in a dish and pour over the marinade. Cover and leave them in the refrigerator for *2 hours*.

3 Preheat the grill and arrange the chicken pieces in the grill pan, making sure they are fairly thickly spread with the marinade. Grill for about *15 minutes*, turning occasionally, until cooked right through. The skin side will take a little longer than the other side.

4 Meanwhile, heat the remaining marinade, adding a little water if it is too thick, to make a sauce.

5 When the chicken is cooked, cut it into slices and arrange them on a warmed serving dish.

6 Serve the chicken garnished with spring onion slivers and diced chilli, with the sauce in a separate bowl.

Serves 4

Thai Curried Chicken Skewers

Preparation time: about 30 minutes, plus marinating
Cooking time: about 14 minutes

- 500 g/1 lb boneless, skinless chicken breast or thighs, cut into 2.5 cm/1 inch pieces
- 1 small green and 1 small red pepper, cored, deseeded and cut into 16 chunks

CURRY MARINADE:
- 2 tablespoons Thai Red Curry Paste
- 1 tablespoon ground coriander
- 2 tablespoons chopped fresh coriander
- 3 tablespoons groundnut oil
- 1 tablespoon ground cumin
- 2 teaspoons soft brown sugar
- 1 lemon grass stalk, very finely chopped (optional)
- 4 tablespoons lime juice

TO GARNISH:
- lime wedges
- coriander sprigs

1 Place all the ingredients for the curry marinade in a non-metallic bowl and mix well to combine. Add the chicken pieces to the marinade and turn them so they are evenly coated. Cover the bowl and leave to marinate in the refrigerator for *2 hours*.

2 Thread the marinated chicken on to 8 presoaked wooden or oiled metal skewers, alternating them with the pepper chunks. Reserve any remaining marinade.

3 Cook the chicken skewers under a preheated medium hot grill for about *7 minutes* on each side, basting them with the reserved marinade whilst they are cooking.

4 Serve the chicken at once, garnished with lime wedges and coriander sprigs.

Serves 4

Thai Red Curry Paste

The heat of this paste depends on the heat of the chillies used. If you want a really hot curry paste, include a few of the seeds from the chillies.

Preparation time: 15 minutes
Cooking time: 5 minutes

- 1 tablespoon chopped fresh coriander
- 1 tablespoon ground coriander
- ½ tablespoon ground cumin
- ½ teaspoon turmeric
- ½ teaspoon black peppercorns
- ½ teaspoon salt
- 1 teaspoon shrimp paste (optional)
- 1 lemon grass stalk, finely chopped (optional)
- 2 garlic cloves, finely chopped
- 5 large red chillies, deseeded and finely chopped
- 2.5 cm/1 inch piece of galangal or root ginger, finely chopped
- 1½ tablespoons oil

1 Place all the ingredients except the groundnut oil in a food processor or blender and purée to a smooth, thick paste. Alternatively, crush the ingredients in a large mortar.

2 Heat the oil in a heavy-based frying pan, add the curry paste and fry over a gentle heat, stirring, for about *5 minutes* until the curry paste is fragrant.

3 Leave the curry paste to cool completely and store in an air-tight jar in the refrigerator. Use as required. The paste will keep for about *2–3 weeks*.

Grilled Chicken Creole

Preparation time: 10 minutes, plus marinating
Cooking time: 15–20 minutes
Oven temperature: 200°C (400°F), Gas Mark 6

- 6 skinless, boneless, chicken breasts
- salt and pepper

SEASONING:

- 2 spring onions, finely chopped
- ½ red onion, finely chopped
- 2 garlic cloves, crushed
- 1 fresh red chilli, deseeded and finely chopped
- 3 chives, snipped
- few thyme sprigs, chopped
- few parsley sprigs, chopped
- 3 allspice berries, crushed (optional)

- 2 tablespoons lime juice
- 2 tablespoons olive oil

AVOCADO SAUCE:

- 1 large ripe avocado, halved, stoned and peeled
- 1 tablespoon finely chopped onion
- ½ garlic clove, crushed
- cayenne pepper, to taste
- lime juice (optional)

TO GARNISH:

- red basil leaves (optional)
- coriander sprigs

1 First prepare the seasoning. Put the spring onions, onion, garlic, chilli, herbs and allspice berries (if using) in a bowl. Add the lime juice and olive oil and stir well to mix thoroughly.

2 Slash the chicken breasts 2–3 times on both sides, and season lightly with salt and pepper. Rub the seasoning over both sides of each chicken breast, pressing it into the slashes. Cover and chill in the refrigerator for *2–3 hours*.

3 Put the chicken breasts on a grill pan and cook under a preheated hot grill, turning once, until cooked on both sides. Take care that the herbs do not burn. Alternatively, cook them in a preheated oven, 200°C (400°F), Gas Mark 6, for about *20 minutes*.

4 While the chicken is cooking, make the avocado sauce. Mash the avocado to a smooth paste and beat in the onion, garlic and a little cayenne pepper. Add a little lime juice, if wished. This will prevent the sauce discolouring. Serve piped on to the plate with the grilled chicken and some saffron rice.

Serves 4

Chicken Calypso

Preparation time: 10 minutes
Cooking time: 50 minutes

- 5 tablespoons groundnut oil
- 2 kg/4 lb chicken, cut into pieces
- 500 g/1 lb long-grain rice
- 1 onion, finely chopped
- 1 green pepper, cored, deseeded and finely chopped
- ½ teaspoon saffron threads (optional)
- 600 ml/1 pint Chicken Stock (see page 8)
- 5 cm/2 inch piece of lime rind
- 1 tablespoon rum
- dash of Angostura bitters
- 125 g/4 oz mushrooms, sliced
- salt and pepper

1 Heat 3 tablespoons of the oil in a large, heavy frying pan and add the chicken pieces. Fry them until they are golden brown all over, turning them occasionally. Remove the chicken and keep warm.

2 Add the rice, onion and green pepper to the pan, and stir well. Fry gently until the rice grains are translucent. Stir in the saffron (if using), chicken stock, lime rind, rum and Angostura bitters.

3 Transfer the rice and vegetable mixture to a heavy flameproof casserole dish, and place the chicken pieces on top. Season well with salt and pepper.

4 Heat the remaining oil in a clean pan and fry the mushrooms for *5 minutes*. Add to the casserole then cover and simmer gently for about *30 minutes*, until the chicken is cooked and all the liquid absorbed. Remove the lid for the last *5 minutes* so that the rice is light and fluffy. Serve hot.

Serves 4–6

Pasta with Chicken, Cream and Mushrooms

Use white button mushrooms for this sauce – dark ones will spoil its delicate appearance.

Preparation time: 30 minutes
Cooking time: 30 minutes

- 3 part-boned chicken breasts
- 1 small onion, quartered
- 1 carrot, roughly chopped
- 1 bouquet garni
- few black peppercorns
- 300 ml/½ pint water
- 2 tablespoons dry sherry (optional)
- 50 g/2 oz butter
- 250 g/8 oz button mushrooms, thinly sliced
- 2 garlic cloves, crushed
- 1 teaspoon chopped rosemary
- 1 tablespoon extra virgin olive oil
- 375 g/12 oz dried pasta shapes (such as farfalle, penne or fusilli)
- 1½ tablespoons plain flour
- 150 ml/¼ pint double cream
- salt and pepper

TO GARNISH:

- rosemary sprigs
- lemon wedges

1 Put the chicken in a saucepan with the onion, carrot, bouquet garni and peppercorns. Pour in the water, and add the sherry, if using.

2 Bring to the boil, then lower the heat, cover and poach the chicken for about *20 minutes* until just tender when pierced with a skewer or fork.

3 Meanwhile, melt the butter in a separate pan, add the mushrooms, garlic, rosemary and salt and pepper to taste, and sauté over a moderate heat, stirring frequently, for about *5 minutes*. Transfer the mushrooms from the liquid to a bowl.

4 Bring a large saucepan of water to the boil, swirl in the oil and add ½ teaspoon salt. Add the pasta and boil, uncovered, over a moderate heat for *10 minutes*, or according to packet instructions, until al dente.

5 Meanwhile, lift the chicken out of the poaching liquid, then strain the liquid into a jug. Cut the chicken into strips, discarding the skin and bones.

6 Return the mushroom cooking liquid to the heat, sprinkle in the flour and cook for *1–2 minutes*, stirring. Add the chicken poaching liquid a little at a time, beating vigorously after each addition.

7 Bring to the boil, stirring. Lower the heat and add the chicken, mushrooms, cream and seasoning. Stir well, then simmer, stirring frequently, for *5 minutes* until thickened.

8 Drain the pasta and turn into a warmed serving bowl. Pour in the sauce and toss to mix with the pasta. Serve garnished with rosemary and a wedge of lemon.

Serves 4

variation
Pasta with Chicken, Cream and Courgettes

Preparation time: 30 minutes
Cooking time: 30 minutes

1 Substitute 2 courgettes, cut into neat batons, for the mushrooms. Continue as in the main recipe.

Basque-style Chicken

Preparation time: 20 minutes
Cooking time: 1 hour

- 175 g/6 oz smoked ham or streaky bacon, diced
- 4 tablespoons olive oil
- 4 large chicken pieces
- 4 onions, sliced
- 3 garlic cloves, crushed
- 2 green peppers, deseeded and diced
- ½ teaspoon dried marjoram
- 400 g/13 oz fresh or canned tomatoes
- 150–300 ml/¼–½ pint Chicken Stock (see page 8)
- salt and pepper
- 2 tablespoons chopped parsley, to garnish

1 Fry the ham or bacon in the oil until lightly browned, then remove with a slotted spoon. Add the chicken and cook until brown all over. Remove the chicken, add the onions, garlic, peppers and marjoram, cover and cook gently for *10 minutes*.

2 Add the tomatoes, seasoning and stock (300 ml/½ pint if using fresh tomatoes; 150 ml/¼ pint if canned). Return the chicken and ham to the pan, cover and simmer for *40–45 minutes*, until the chicken is cooked and tender.

3 Transfer the chicken to a serving dish. Boil the sauce to thicken slightly, pour over the chicken and sprinkle with chopped parsley.

Serves 4

variation _____

Creamy Paprika Chicken

Preparation time: 20 minutes
Cooking time: 1 hour

1 Substitute red peppers for the green peppers and follow steps 1 and 2 of the main recipe, adding 1 tablespoon of paprika when you return the chicken and ham to the sauce.

2 Transfer the chicken to a serving dish. Boil the sauce to thicken slightly, then stir in 150 ml/¼ pint soured cream. Stir well, then heat gently until warmed through. Pour the sauce over the chicken and sprinkle with chopped parsley.

Serves 4

Chicken Breasts en Croûte

Preparation time: 30 minutes
Cooking time: about 40 minutes
Oven temperature: 200°C (400°F), Gas Mark 6

- 2 tablespoons extra virgin olive oil
- 125 g/4 oz brown cap mushrooms, finely chopped
- 2 garlic cloves, crushed
- 2 teaspoons chopped thyme
- 6 large skinless, boneless chicken breasts
- 125 g/4 oz pâté de campagne

- 2 tablespoons sherry or brandy
- 425 g/14 oz puff pastry
- salt and pepper
- beaten egg, to glaze

TO GARNISH:

- sautéed mushroom slices
- thyme sprigs

1 Heat the oil in a small frying pan, add the mushrooms and sauté over a moderate heat, stirring frequently, for about *5 minutes* until the juices run.

2 Increase the heat to high and stir the mushrooms until all of the liquid has evaporated and the mushrooms are quite dry.

3 Add the garlic, thyme and salt and pepper to taste and cook for a further *5 minutes*. Remove from the heat and leave to cool.

4 Make a long horizontal slit through the thickest part of each chicken breast without cutting right through.

5 Soften the pâté in a bowl with the sherry or brandy, then beat in the mushroom mixture until evenly combined. Spread the pâté inside the cavities in the chicken breasts, dividing it equally between them, then close the chicken tightly around the stuffing.

6 Roll out the pastry on a floured work surface and cut out 6 squares large enough to enclose the chicken breasts. Brush the edges of the pastry with water.

7 Place a stuffed chicken breast in the centre of each pastry square, then bring up the pastry around the chicken to form a parcel. Brush the seams with more water and press together well to seal.

8 Put the chicken parcels, seam-side down, on a moistened baking sheet. Roll out the pastry trimmings and cut out small decorative shapes. Brush the parcels all over with beaten egg, then press the decorative shapes on top. Brush the shapes with beaten egg.

9 Bake in a preheated oven, 200°C (400°F), Gas Mark 6, for *30 minutes* or until the pastry is golden and the chicken feels tender when pierced in the centre with a skewer. Serve hot, garnished with a few sautéed mushroom slices and thyme sprigs. A juicy vegetable dish, such as ratatouille, would make a good accompaniment, as would new potatoes.

Serves 6

Chicken stuffed with Spinach and Ricotta

Preparation time: 5 minutes
Cooking time: 25 minutes
Oven temperature: 200°C (400°F), Gas Mark 6

- **4 skinless, boneless, chicken breasts**
- **125 g/4 oz ricotta cheese**
- **125 g/4 oz cooked spinach, squeezed dry**
- **¼ teaspoon grated nutmeg**
- **8 slices Parma ham**

- **2 tablespoons olive oil, plus extra for drizzling**
- **salt and pepper**

TO SERVE:
- **rocket leaves with olive oil**
- **lemon wedges**

1 Make a long horizontal slit through the thickest part of each chicken breast without cutting right through.

2 Crumble the ricotta into a bowl. Chop the spinach and mix into the ricotta with the nutmeg. Season with salt and pepper.

3 Divide the stuffing between the slits in the chicken breasts and wrap each one in 2 pieces of Parma ham, winding it around the chicken to totally cover the meat.

4 Heat the oil in a shallow ovenproof pan, add the chicken breasts and sauté for *4 minutes* on each side or until the ham starts to brown. Transfer to a preheated oven, 200°C (400°F), Gas Mark 6, and cook for *15 minutes*. Serve with a wedge of lemon and rocket leaves drizzled with olive oil.

Serves 4

variation

Chicken with Mozzarella and Sun-dried Tomatoes

Preparation time: 5 minutes
Cooking time: 25 minutes

1 Instead of the ricotta, spinach and nutmeg, stuff each chicken breast with a thick slice of mozzarella and a sun-dried tomato piece, drained of its olive oil. Season well with black pepper and continue as in the main recipe.

Chicken, Squash and Sweet Potato Tagine

Squash and sweet potatoes and just one spice, cinnamon, make this a mild, soothing tagine. Some of the parsley and mint are reserved to add at the end to give a bit of zip to the flavour, and flaked almonds are scattered over for a contrast in texture.

Preparation time: 20 minutes
Cooking time: 1 hour

- 2 tablespoons olive oil
- 1.5 kg/3 lb chicken, cut into 12 pieces
- 2 large onions, finely chopped
- 4 garlic cloves, crushed
- 2 cinnamon sticks, broken in half
- 500 g/1 lb sweet potatoes, cut into small cubes
- 500 g/1 lb squash or pumpkin, cut into small cubes
- small handful of chopped mixed parsley and mint
- 300 ml/½ pint Chicken Stock (see page 8)
- salt and pepper

TO GARNISH:
- flaked almonds
- parsley sprigs
- mint sprigs

1 Heat the oil in a large heavy casserole. Add the chicken in batches and brown evenly. Remove and keep warm. Add the onions to the casserole and cook until soft and lightly browned, adding the garlic and cinnamon when the onions are nearly done.

2 Stir in the sweet potatoes and squash or pumpkin, then return the chicken to the pan, add half of the parsley and mint and pour in the stock. Cover tightly and simmer very gently for about *45 minutes* until the chicken and vegetables are tender.

3 Season to taste with salt and pepper then add the remaining parsley and mint. Scatter over the almonds and serve garnished with parsley and mint sprigs and the broken cinnamon sticks.

Serves 4

Chicken and Ham Cannelloni

Preparation time: 30 minutes
Cooking time: 1½ hours
Oven temperature: 190°C (375°F), Gas Mark 5

- 2 tablespoons oil
- 1 small onion, finely chopped
- 175 g/6 oz skinless, boneless chicken, minced
- 125 g/4 oz lean ham, finely chopped
- 65 g/2½ oz full-fat soft cheese with garlic and herbs
- 8 no-need-to-precook cannelloni tubes
- 3 tablespoons grated Parmesan cheese
- salt and pepper
- flat leaf parsley sprigs, to garnish

TOMATO SAUCE:

- 1 tablespoon olive oil
- 1 large onion, finely chopped
- 2 garlic cloves, crushed
- 400 g/13 oz can chopped tomatoes
- 2 teaspoons sugar
- 3 tablespoons tomato puree
- 150 ml/¼ pint water or Chicken Stock (see page 8)
- 1 teaspoon dried mixed herbs

1 First prepare the sauce. Heat the oil in a pan. Add the onion and garlic and cook over a moderate heat until soft but not brown. Add the remaining ingredients. Bring to the boil, stirring occasionally. Lower the heat, cover and simmer for *40 minutes*.

2 To make the filling, heat the oil in a frying pan. Add the onion and fry over a moderate heat until soft but not brown. Add the chicken and cook for a few minutes, until just cooked. Remove from the heat. Stir in the ham and soft cheese with salt and pepper to taste. Mix well and use to fill the cannelloni tubes.

3 Place the filled cannelloni in a lightly greased ovenproof dish, pour over the prepared tomato sauce and sprinkle with the Parmesan. Bake in the centre of a preheated oven, 190°C (375°F), Gas Mark 5 for *40 minutes*. Serve immediately garnished with sprigs of flat leaf parsley.

Serves 4

variation

Chicken and Artichoke Cannelloni

Preparation time: 30 minutes
Cooking time: 1½ hours
Oven temperature: 190°C (375°F), Gas Mark 5

- 2 tablespoons oil
- 1 small onion, finely chopped
- 175 g/6 oz skinless, boneless chicken, minced
- 200 g/7 oz artichoke hearts in olive oil, drained and chopped
- 65 g/2½ oz full-fat soft cheese
- handful of basil leaves, chopped
- 8 no-need-to-precook cannelloni tubes
- 3 tablespoons grated Parmesan cheese
- salt and pepper
- flat leaf parsley sprigs, to garnish
- 1 quantity Tomato Sauce (see main recipe)

1 Follow the main recipe to make the tomato sauce.

2 To make the filling, heat the oil in a frying pan. Add the onion and fry over a moderate heat until soft but not brown. Add the chicken and cook for a few minutes, until just cooked. Remove from the heat. Stir in the artichoke hearts, soft cheese and basil, with salt and pepper to taste. Mix well and use to fill the cannelloni tubes.

3 Follow the main recipe to cook and serve the cannelloni.

Serves 4

Special Occasions

Prepare an impressive dish that will rise to any occasion with these exciting recipes. Sophisticated, yet deceptively quick to prepare, the results will surprise and delight, ensuring that every occasion will be a success whether you are preparing an intimate meal for two or catering for a larger party.

Pan-fried Chicken Breasts with Sun-dried Tomatoes and Grapes

Preparation time: 10 minutes
Cooking time: 35 minutes

- 3 tablespoons olive oil
- 4 part-boned skinless
  chicken breasts
- 1 red onion, thinly sliced
- 2 garlic cloves, crushed
- 75 g/3 oz sun-dried
  tomatoes in oil, thinly sliced
- 1 tablespoon plain flour
- 300 ml/½ pint dry white wine
- 150 ml/¼ pint Chicken Stock
  (see page 8)
- 1 teaspoon chopped
  oregano
- 150 g/5 oz seedless grapes,
  halved if large
- salt and pepper
- oregano sprigs, to garnish

1 Heat the oil in a large sauté pan, add the chicken, in batches if necessary, and sauté over a moderate heat for *7–10 minutes*, until golden on both sides. Remove with a slotted spoon and set aside on a plate.

2 Add the onion and garlic to the pan and fry over a gentle heat, stirring frequently, for about *5 minutes* until softened but not coloured. Add the sun-dried tomatoes and stir well to combine, then add the flour and cook for *1–2 minutes*, stirring. Add the wine, stock, oregano and salt and pepper to taste. Bring to the boil, stirring all the time.

3 Return the chicken to the pan with the juices that have collected on the plate, and stir well to mix. Cover the pan and simmer over a gentle heat for *20 minutes*, turning the chicken and basting it occasionally with the sauce, until it is tender when pierced with a skewer.

4 Add the grapes and stir to mix into the sauce. Heat through gently for *1–2 minutes*, then taste for seasoning. Serve hot, sliced and garnished with sprigs of oregano.

Serves 4

variation

Chicken Paprikash

Preparation time: 30 minutes
Cooking time: about 50 minutes

1 Heat 3 tablespoons olive oil in a large flameproof casserole. Sauté 4 skinless chicken breasts over a moderate heat for *7–10 minutes* until golden. Remove and set aside.

2 Heat 1½ tablespoons oil in the casserole, add 1 large thinly sliced onion, 1 crushed garlic clove, 2 tablespoons sweet Hungarian paprika and a large pinch of sugar. Cook gently, stirring frequently, for *10–15 minutes* until the onion is soft.

3 Add 1 tablespoon tomato purée and 6 large ripe tomatoes, skinned, deseeded, and chopped, and stir well. Add 200 ml/ 7 fl oz chicken stock and salt and pepper to taste. Bring to the boil, stirring. Add the chicken and its juices, cover and simmer over a gentle heat, stirring occasionally, for *40 minutes* or until the chicken is cooked. Check the seasoning.

4 Serve hot. Buttered noodles tossed in caraway or poppy seeds are the traditional accompaniment.

Serves 4

Chicken with Wild Mushrooms

Preparation time: 5 minutes
Cooking time: 25 minutes

- 50 g/2 oz dried wild
  mushrooms or 250 g/8 oz
  fresh mushrooms, sliced
- 50 g/2 oz plain flour
- 4 skinless, boneless chicken
  breasts
- 50 g/2 oz butter
- 1 tablespoon olive oil
- 2 shallots, diced
- 2 garlic cloves, chopped
- 125 ml/4 fl oz white wine
- 125 g/4 oz mascarpone
  cheese
- handful of chives, snipped,
  plus extra to garnish
- salt and pepper

1 If using dried mushrooms, put them into a bowl and just cover with hot water. Leave to soak for *15 minutes*.

2 Meanwhile, season the flour with salt and pepper and toss the chicken in the seasoned flour to cover all over.

3 Heat the butter and oil in a frying pan, add the chicken and cook on each side for *4 minutes* or until golden. Remove the chicken and keep warm.

4 Add the shallots and garlic to the pan and sauté gently for *5 minutes*. Add the wine and mix well to include any tasty brown bits from the pan.

5 Add the mascarpone and the mushrooms to the pan; if using wild mushrooms, add the soaking liquid. Mix well to melt the mascarpone. If the mixture is very runny, turn up the heat to evaporate some of the liquid. If you are using fresh mushrooms, add a little extra liquid, but mushrooms make their own liquid as they cook.

6 Return the chicken to the pan and simmer gently for *10 minutes*, turning it occasionally. Finally stir the chives into the pan and serve immediately, garnished with chives.

Serves 4

Char-grilled Poussins with Sweet Potatoes and Red Lentils

Preparation time: 30 minutes, plus marinating
Cooking time: 1 hour

- 4 x 500 g/1 lb poussins, spatchcocked (see page 7)
- 4 tablespoons sunflower oil
- 50 g/2 oz shallots, grated
- 2 garlic cloves, crushed
- 50 g/2 oz carrot, grated
- 200 g/7 oz red lentils
- 200 ml/7 fl oz Chicken Stock (see page 8)
- 4 teaspoons Thai Red Curry Paste (see page 58)
- 300 g/10 oz sweet potatoes, diced
- 1 teaspoon cumin seeds
- small handful of coriander leaves, chopped
- salt and pepper

MARINADE:
- 4 tablespoons Dijon mustard
- 6 garlic cloves, crushed
- 125 ml/4 fl oz sunflower oil
- few rosemary sprigs

TO GARNISH:
- olive oil
- 1 lemon, quartered
- rosemary sprigs

1 To make the marinade, put the Dijon mustard and garlic into a food processor or blender. Blend, then slowly pour in the sunflower oil to form a smooth paste. Transfer the paste to shallow dish and add the rosemary.

2 Turn the spatchcocked poussins in the mustard mixture, cover and leave to marinate in the refrigerator for *24 hours*.

3 Heat 2 tablespoons of the oil in a large saucepan, add the shallots, garlic, carrot and lentils and turn in the oil. Add half the stock and bring to the boil. Reduce the heat and simmer gently, adding more stock, a ladleful at a time, until all the stock has been used and the lentils are cooked. Stir in the curry paste and season to taste with salt and pepper. Cover and set aside.

4 Heat the remaining oil in another saucepan, add the sweet potatoes and cumin seeds and fry for *7–10* minutes until the sweet potatoes are soft but not coloured.

5 Remove the poussins from the marinade and cook under a preheated hot grill or on a barbecue for *10 minutes* on each side, until tender and cooked right through.

6 Meanwhile, gently reheat the lentil mixture and stir in the sweet potatoes and coriander. To serve, divide the lentil and sweet potato mixture between four warmed plates, place the poussins on top and drizzle with a little olive oil. Garnish with the lemon quarters and the rosemary sprigs and serve hot.

Serves 4

Chicken with Oyster Mushrooms, Garlic and Crème Fraîche

Delicate oyster mushrooms are excellent for making sauces.

Preparation time: 20 minutes
Cooking time: about 40 minutes

- 125 g/4 oz smoked streaky bacon rashers, derinded and cut into strips
- 15 g/½ oz butter
- 6 large skinless chicken breasts
- 1 tablespoon plain flour
- 300 ml/½ pint dry white wine

- 175 g/6 oz oyster mushrooms, thinly sliced, plus extra to garnish
- 1 garlic clove, crushed
- 75 ml/3 fl oz crème fraîche, plus extra to serve
- ½ teaspoon chopped rosemary
- salt and pepper
- rosemary sprigs, to garnish

1 Fry the strips of bacon gently in a large flameproof casserole, stirring, for about *5 minutes* until the fat runs. Add the butter and, when melted, sauté the chicken over a moderate heat for about *5 minutes* until golden on all sides.

2 Sprinkle in the flour and turn the chicken to cover all over, then gradually stir in the wine and bring to the boil, stirring. Add the mushrooms, garlic and crème fraîche with the rosemary and plenty of pepper.

3 Stir well, then cover and simmer gently for *25 minutes* or until the chicken is tender when pierced with a skewer or fork. Turn and baste it frequently.

4 Taste the sauce for seasoning. Slice the chicken and garnish each portion with fresh rosemary, an oyster mushroom and some crème fraîche.

Serves 6

variation
Chicken with Asparagus

Preparation time: 20 minutes
Cooking time: about 40 minutes

1 Follow steps 1–3 of the main recipe, omitting the oyster mushrooms.

2 Meanwhile, boil or steam 75 g/3 oz asparagus tips briefly until just tender. Drain, refresh under cold running water, and drain again thoroughly.

3 Stir the asparagus tips into the sauce and heat through. Taste the sauce for seasoning. Slice the chicken and garnish each portion with fresh rosemary, an asparagus tip and some crème fraîche.

Serves 6

Braised Poussin with Calvados

Preparation time: 10 minutes
Cooking time: about 1¼ hours

- 4 poussins
- 25 g/1 oz butter
- 2 tablespoons olive oil
- 4 back bacon rashers, derinded and chopped
- 4 carrots, quartered
- 1 large onion, quartered
- 4 tablespoons Calvados
- 2 Russet or Cox's apples, peeled, cored and sliced
- 3–4 thyme sprigs, chopped
- 300 ml/½ pint dry cider
- 150 ml/5 fl oz double cream
- salt and pepper
- deep-fried thyme sprigs, to garnish

1 Sprinkle the poussins liberally, inside and out, with salt and pepper. Heat the butter and oil in a large flameproof casserole, add the poussins and cook for *15 minutes*, until golden brown all over, finishing with the breast upwards. Add the bacon, carrots and onion for the last *5 minutes*.

2 Warm the Calvados in a ladle over a gentle heat, pour over the poussins and set alight. When the flames have subsided, add the apples, thyme and cider. Cover and simmer gently for *1 hour*, spooning the liquid over the breast occasionally. Transfer the poussins to a warmed serving dish; keep warm.

3 Boil the cooking liquid briskly until reduced by half. Add the cream and heat gently, stirring until smooth. Pour the sauce over the poussins.

4 Serve, garnished with the thyme sprigs, and with crusty French bread, if liked.

Serves 4

Honey-Glazed Poussins

Preparation time: 10 minutes, plus marinating
Cooking time: 45 minutes
Oven temperature: 200°C (400°F), Gas Mark 6

- 1 tablespoon thick honey
- 2 garlic cloves, crushed
- 3–4 tablespoons wine vinegar
- 1 tablespoon chopped marjoram

- 4 poussins
- sprig of marjoram, to garnish

TO SERVE:

- crystallised honey
- baby gem lettuce
- fresh peaches, sliced

1 Mix together the honey, garlic and vinegar in a large dish. Put a little marjoram inside each poussin, place in the dish and turn in the marinade to cover all over. Cover and marinate in the refrigerator for *2 hours,* turning occasionally.

2 Lift the birds out of the marinade, place in a roasting tin and roast in a preheated oven, 200°C (400°F), Gas Mark 6, for *30 minutes*. Cover with foil and cook for *15 minutes* more.

3 Garnish with a sprig of marjoram and serve with a baby gem and peach salad, and some crystallised honey.

Serves 4

variation
Lemon-Thyme Poussins

Preparation time: 10 minutes, plus marinating
Cooking time: 45 minutes
Oven temperature: 200°C (400°F), Gas Mark 6

1 As an alternative marinade, mix together the juice and finely grated rind of 2 lemons, 1 tablespoon thick honey and 2 crushed garlic cloves. Put 2 thyme sprigs inside each bird and follow the main recipe for marinating, cooking and serving the poussins.

Serves 4

Broccoli and Coriander Chicken

Preparation time: 10 minutes
Cooking time: about 1 hour
Oven temperature   200°C (400°F), Gas Mark 6

- 4 skinless, boneless chicken breasts
- 600 ml/1 pint Chicken Stock (see page 8)
- 750 g/1½ lb broccoli
- coriander sprigs, to garnish

SAUCE:
- 50 g/2 oz butter
- 1 large onion, finely chopped
- 3 garlic cloves, crushed
- 2–3 tablespoons Mild Curry Paste (see page 56) or shop-bought curry paste

- 750 ml/1¼ pints crème fraîche
- 1½ tablespoons lemon juice
- 3 tablespoons finely chopped coriander
- salt and pepper

GRATIN TOPPING:
- 50 g/2 oz butter
- 125 g/4 oz fresh white breadcrumbs
- 50 g/2 oz mature Cheddar cheese, grated

1 Cut the chicken into strips about 8 x 2 cm/3½ x ¾ inch long. Heat the stock in a saucepan, then poach the chicken strips gently for *4–6 minutes* until just cooked. Remove the chicken from the stock with a slotted spoon and set aside.

2 Trim the broccoli into florets and peel the stalks. Plunge the florets into a large pan of boiling water and cook for *2 minutes*, then drain. Refresh under cold running water until very cold. Drain again and dry with kitchen paper.

3 To make the topping, melt the butter in a large frying pan and gently fry the breadcrumbs until golden brown.

4 To make the sauce, melt the butter in a large saucepan and fry the onion and garlic until soft but not coloured. Stir in the curry paste and fry for *2 minutes* to develop the flavour. Add the crème fraîche, lemon juice and coriander, season to taste with salt and pepper and mix well. Bring the sauce to the boil.

5 Arrange the chicken and broccoli in an ovenproof dish. Pour the hot sauce over the top. Scatter the grated cheese on top followed by the breadcrumbs. Bake in a preheated oven, 200°C (400°F), Gas Mark 6, for about *30–40 minutes* until bubbling hot and golden brown. For a crunchy topping, flash under a preheated grill, if necessary.

Serves 6

variation _____

Cheesy Broccoli and Chicken Gratin

Preparation time: 10 minutes
Cooking time: about 1 hour
Oven temperature: 200°C (400°F), Gas Mark 6

1 Follow steps 1–3 of the main recipe.

2 To make the sauce, melt the butter in a large saucepan and fry the onion and garlic until soft but not coloured. Stir in the crème fraîche, lemon juice, 100 g/3½ oz Cheddar cheese, season to taste with salt and pepper and mix well. Omit the curry paste and coriander from the sauce. Bring the sauce to the boil.

3 Follow step 5 of the main recipe to assemble and cook the gratin.

Serves 6

Chicken with Fennel

Preparation time: 10 minutes
Cooking time: 1¼–1½ hours
Oven temperature: 200°C (400°F), Gas Mark 6

- 1.75 kg/3½ lb chicken
- 175 g/6 oz cooked ham, cut into thick strips
- 2 tablespoons chopped fennel stalks and leaves
- 2 garlic cloves, crushed
- 40 g/1½ oz butter, softened
- lemon juice
- salt and pepper
- fennel leaves, to garnish

1 Season the chicken inside and out with salt and pepper. Mix together the ham, fennel stalks and leaves, and garlic and stuff the chicken. Place in a deep casserole dish and spread the butter over the chicken.

2 Cover the casserole and cook in a preheated oven, 200°C (400°F), Gas Mark 6, for *1 hour*. Remove the lid and continue cooking, basting frequently, for *20 minutes* until tender. Remove the chicken with a slotted spoon and transfer to a warmed serving dish and keep hot.

3 Season the juices with salt, pepper and lemon juice to taste, and reheat. Serve the chicken, garnished with fennel leaves, accompanied by its juices, and Tuscan Baked Fennel.

Serves 4

Tuscan Baked Fennel

The Italians adore fennel and have countless ways of cooking it to serve with meat, poultry and fish. This recipe is popular in Tuscany and is delicious served with chicken.

Preparation time: 5 minutes
Cooking time: 25–30 minutes

- 625 g/1¼ lb fennel bulbs, trimmed and cut vertically into 2 cm/¾ inch pieces
- 1 thick slice of lemon
- 1 tablespoon oil
- 25 g/1 oz butter
- 25 g/1 oz Parmesan cheese, grated
- salt and pepper

1 Put the fennel in a saucepan with a pinch of salt, the lemon and oil and pour in enough boiling water to cover. Cook for *20 minutes* then drain well.

2 Melt the butter in a gratin dish, add the fennel and turn to coat. Season to taste with pepper and sprinkle with the Parmesan cheese. Place under a preheated grill until lightly browned. Serve immediately.

Serves 4

Exotic Ingredients

To give chicken dishes a more unusual flavour or a new twist, look to using more exotic ingredients from all over the world. These are now widely available in supermarkets or specialist stores and will make all the difference to a meal.

Pesto sauce

Coconut milk

Lemon grass

Dried galangal

Chilli dipping sauce

Saffron threads

Pesto sauce is now conveniently available at supermarkets. It is a blend of basil, toasted pine nuts, garlic, Parmesan, lemon juice and lemon rind and can be used in salads as a dressing or in pasta dishes.

Coconut milk is mainly used in Indian cooking and Far East dishes. It adds a distinctive smooth taste to curries, sauces and rice. It can be bought in cans, packets or blocks at supermarkets.

Lemon grass can be bought in bundles of 4–6 stalks. The ends should be trimmed and the stalks thinly sliced. A suitable alternative to lemon grass is lemon rind or juice.

Dried galangal is a root similar to ginger but it has a more mellow taste. It is available fresh or dried at supermarkets or ethnic stores.

Chilli dipping sauce is used as an accompaniment to Chinese and Thai dishes. It works equally well as a dip or a marinade and can be bought in most supermarkets or made at home.

Saffron threads are used in chicken soups, sauces and rice dishes. The threads should be soaked in hot water: they provide a vivid yellow colour and a distinctive flavour.

Green curry paste

Red curry paste

Thai fish sauce (*nam pla*)

Sake

Hoisin sauce

Harissa

Palm sugar

Thai fish sauce (*nam pla*) is generally used in Thai cooking; it is made using fermented salted fish and complements chicken well.

Green curry paste is a combination of green chillies, coriander, lemon grass, cumin, turmeric and garlic. It can be home-made or shop-bought.

Red curry paste is similar to green curry paste but with dried red chillies, paprika and shrimp paste.

Sake is synonymous with Japan, an alcoholic drink made by fermenting steamed white rice. It adds a full flavour to many soups and sauces with chicken. If sake is unavailable, dry sherry can be used instead.

Hoisin sauce is a Chinese sauce often used for marinating chicken; it can also be served as a dipping sauce. Its main ingredient is the soya bean.

Harissa is a chilli paste used in North African cooking, a blend of chillies, roasted red peppers, garlic, toasted coriander seeds and caraway seeds. It can be used as an ingredient or as a condiment; it imparts a rich, strong flavour

Palm sugar is unrefined cane sugar. It is used as a sweetening agent in curries and Indian sauces.

Family Meals

When you have a little more time on your hands, and a couple more mouths to feed, here are some dishes that will amply reward the time you spend on them. Suitably appetizing and full of healthy ingredients, the longer cooking times seal in the wholesome flavours, creating delicious dishes that will satisfy all the members of your family.

Braised Chicken with New Potatoes and Paprika

Preparation time: 25 minutes
Cooking time: 1¼ hours

- 2 tablespoons vegetable oil
- 200 g/7 oz streaky bacon, derinded and cut into strips
- 1.5 kg/3 lb chicken, cut into 8 pieces
- 1 large onion, chopped
- 1 large green pepper, cored, deseeded and chopped
- 1 garlic clove, finely chopped

- 4 tablespoons plain flour
- 2 tablespoons sweet paprika
- 600 ml/1 pint Chicken Stock (see page 8)
- 125 ml/4 fl oz dry white wine
- 12 small new potatoes, halved
- 300 ml/½ pint soured cream
- salt and pepper
- flat leaf parsley, to garnish

1 Heat the oil in a large flameproof casserole over a moderate heat. Add the bacon and cook for *5 minutes*, stirring frequently. Remove the bacon with a slotted spoon and set aside. Pour off all but 3 tablespoons of the fat.

2 Season the chicken. Place in the casserole, skin side down, over a medium-high heat. Brown, turning occasionally, for *10–15 minutes*. Remove the chicken and set aside.

3 Place the onion in the casserole over a moderate heat. Cook, stirring occasionally, for *5 minutes*. Add the green pepper and garlic, then cook for *1 minute*. Blend in 2 tablespoons of the flour and the paprika and cook for *2–3 minutes*, stirring constantly. Using a whisk, gradually blend in the stock and wine. Bring the mixture to the boil and cook until the sauce is smooth and thick.

4 Return the chicken and bacon to the sauce. Arrange the potatoes around the chicken. Cover and cook over a medium-low heat for *30 minutes*. Remove the breast pieces from the casserole and keep warm on a warmed serving platter. Continue cooking the dark meat for another *10 minutes*.

5 Remove the remaining chicken pieces and place on the serving platter, on top of the potatoes.

6 To finish the sauce, reduce the heat to very low. Combine the soured cream and remaining flour in a small bowl until smooth. Using a whisk, stir into the sauce. Cook gently for *2 minutes*. Pour the sauce over the chicken and potatoes and garnish with flat leaf parsley.

Serves 4

Chicken and Mushroom Pie

Preparation time: 25 minutes
Cooking time: 1¾ hours
Oven temperature: 190°C (375°F), Gas Mark 5

- 1.5 kg/3 lb chicken with giblets
- 1 bouquet garni
- 1 small onion, quartered
- 6–8 black peppercorns
- 25 g/1 oz butter
- 2 leeks, trimmed and thinly sliced
- 125 g/4 oz button mushrooms, sliced
- 1 teaspoon plain flour
- 125 g/4 oz full-fat soft cheese
- 2 tablespoons chopped parsley
- salt
- sprigs of parsley, to garnish

TOPPING:
- 500 g/1 lb potatoes
- 250 g/8 oz carrots, sliced
- 25 g/1 oz butter
- 1 egg
- pinch of grated nutmeg
- pepper

1 Put the chicken and giblets in a large saucepan with the bouquet garni, onion, salt to taste and peppercorns. Cover with water, bring to the boil and skim. Cover the pan and simmer for about 1 *hour*, or until the chicken is cooked. To test, pierce it through the thickest part of the leg with a fine skewer. The juices should run clear.

2 Lift out the chicken and, when it is cool enough to handle, skin it and cut the meat from the bones. Slice the liver. Place the chicken in an ovenproof dish and set aside. Reserve the chicken stock for another recipe or for making soup.

3 Melt the butter in a small pan and fry the leeks and mushrooms over a moderate heat for *3 minutes*, stirring. Stir in the flour, then the cheese and parsley. Simmer for *3 minutes*, then spread the vegetables over the chicken.

4 To make the topping, cook the potatoes and carrots in boiling salted water for *15–20 minutes,* or until they are tender. Drain and mash them and beat in the butter and egg. Season to taste with nutmeg, salt and pepper.

5 Spread the potato topping evenly over the chicken, then fork it up into peaks.

6 Bake in a preheated oven, 190°C (375°F), Gas Mark 5, for *20–25 minutes* until the topping is well browned. Garnish with parsley and serve hot.

Serves 6

Pot Roast Chicken

Preparation time: 10 minutes
Cooking time: 1 hour 10 minutes
Oven temperature: 180°C (350°F), Gas Mark 4

- 1 tablespoon dripping or oil
- 1 onion, sliced
- 2 carrots, sliced
- 1 courgette, sliced
- 1 teaspoon chopped thyme leaves
- 1.25 kg/2½ lb chicken

- 150 ml/¼ pint cider or Chicken Stock (see page 8)
- salt and pepper

TO GARNISH:
- thyme sprigs
- lemon wedges

1 Heat the dripping or oil in an ovenproof casserole. Add the onion and carrots and fry until softened but not brown. Lay the courgettes on the vegetables, season well with salt and pepper and sprinkle on the thyme. Season the chicken and place on top of the vegetables, pushing it well down. Pour the cider or stock over the chicken.

2 Cover and cook in a preheated oven, 180° C (350°F), Gas Mark 4, for *30 minutes*. Baste the chicken and continue cooking for *15 minutes*. Remove the lid and cook for *15 minutes* more, until the chicken is tender and golden.

3 Serve on a warmed dish with the vegetables, garnished with thyme and lemon, with the cooking juices as a sauce.

Serves 3

variation
Cinnamon Roast Chicken

Preparation time: 10 minutes
Cooking time: 1 hour 10 minutes

- 1 tablespoon dripping or oil
- 1 onion, sliced
- 1 butternut squash, peeled and cubed
- 2 teaspoons ground cinnamon
- 1.25 kg/2½ lb chicken

- 150 ml/¼ pint cider or Chicken Stock (see page 8)
- 2 tablespoons lemon juice
- salt and pepper
- lemon wedges, to garnish

1 Heat the dripping or oil in an ovenproof casserole. Add the onion and squash and fry until soft but not brown. Add the cinnamon and season with salt and pepper. Season the chicken and place in the casserole, pushing it well down. Pour the cider or stock and lemon juice over the chicken.

2 Follow steps 2 and 3 of the main recipe to finish the dish.

Serves 3

Stuffed Roast Chicken

Preparation time: 15–20 minutes
Cooking time: about 1¾ hours
Oven temperature: 190°C (375°F), Gas Mark 5

- 2 kg/4 lb chicken
- salt and pepper
- flat leaf parsley, to garnish

STUFFING:

- 40 g/1½ oz butter
- 1 small onion, finely chopped
- 1 celery stick, finely chopped
- 75 g/3 oz wholemeal breadcrumbs
- 25 g/1 oz raisins
- 1 tablespoon chopped parsley
- grated rind of 1 lemon
- 1 tablespoon lemon juice

1 To make the stuffing, melt 15 g/½ oz of the butter in a small pan over a moderate heat and gently fry the onion and celery for *4–5 minutes*, until soft but not brown.

2 Mix the vegetables in a bowl with the breadcrumbs, raisins, half the parsley and half the grated lemon rind. Bind the stuffing together with half the lemon juice and pack it into the chicken. Tie the chicken legs up with string to secure them if necessary. Place on a roasting rack in a roasting tin.

3 Melt the remaining butter or margarine over a low heat in a small pan. Stir in the remaining parsley, lemon rind and lemon juice. Season lightly. Use to baste the chicken.

4 Roast the chicken in a preheated oven, 190°C (375°F), Gas Mark 5, for about 1½ hours, until the juices run clear. Baste with the lemon and parsley mixture several times during the cooking time.

5 When the chicken is cooked, remove the string and place the chicken on a warmed serving dish. Serve the chicken with roasted root vegetables, if liked. Garnish with flat leaf parsley.

Serves 4

Chicken in Peanut Sauce

Preparation time: 5 minutes
Cooking time: 1¼ hours
Oven temperature: 180°C (350°F), Gas Mark 4

- 5 tablespoons oil
- 1 onion, peeled and diced
- 2 tablespoons plain flour
- 4 chicken joints
- 150 ml/¼ pint Chicken Stock (see page 8)
- 150 ml/¼ pint milk
- 1 tablespoon peanut butter
- 1 tablespoon chopped parsley
- 2 tablespoons single cream
- salt and pepper
- parsley sprigs, to garnish

1 Heat the oil in a frying pan and cook the onion for a few minutes until soft but not brown. Transfer to a casserole. Season the flour and coat the chicken well, then fry in the oil until golden brown. Transfer to the casserole.

2 Add the stock to the frying pan, stir well to scrape up the sediment, then add the milk, peanut butter and chopped parsley and bring to the boil, stirring. Pour over the chicken.

3 Cover the casserole and cook in a preheated oven, 180°F (350°C), Gas Mark 4, for *1 hour*. Taste and adjust the seasoning if necessary.

4 Stir in the cream and turn each piece of chicken to coat with the sauce. Serve hot, garnished with parsley.

Serves 4

variation
Chicken in Tomato Sauce

Preparation time: 5 minutes
Cooking time: 1¼ hours
Oven temperature: 180°C (350°F), Gas Mark 4

- 5 tablespoons oil
- 2 tablespoons plain flour
- 4 chicken joints
- 1 onion, peeled and diced
- 400 g/13 oz can chopped tomatoes
- 1 teaspoon sugar
- 2 bay leaves
- 2 tablespoons single cream
- salt and pepper
- parsley sprigs, to garnish

1 Heat the oil in a frying pan. Season the flour and coat the chicken well, then fry in the oil until golden brown. Transfer to an ovenproof casserole.

2 Add the onion to the frying pan and cook gently until soft, but not brown. Turn up the heat and add the tomatoes, sugar and bay leaves. Pour over the chicken and follow steps 3 and 4 of the main recipe to finish the dish.

Serves 4

Chicken with Vegetables, Noodles and Cashew Nuts

Preparation time: 10 minutes
Cooking time: 10–15 minutes

- 50 ml/2 fl oz sunflower oil
- 1 tablespoon light sesame seed oil
- 750 g/1½ lb skinless, boneless chicken breast, cut into thin strips
- 1 large carrot, cut into thin strips
- 2 large peppers, cored, deseeded and cut into strips
- 175 g/6 oz mangetout
- 175 g/6 oz baby sweetcorn
- 375 g/12 oz medium egg noodles, cooked and drained
- 75 g/3 oz cashew nuts, toasted

- 2 spring onions, thinly sliced
- coriander leaves, to garnish

SAUCE:

- 1½ tablespoons cornflour
- 3 garlic cloves, chopped
- 2 teaspoons finely grated fresh root ginger
- 3 tablespoons dark soft brown sugar
- 6 tablespoons dark soy sauce
- 1 teaspoon Tabasco sauce
- 450 ml/¾ pint Chicken Stock (see page 8)

1 First combine all the ingredients for the sauce in a jug, gradually adding the stock to make a smooth liquid.

2 Combine the sunflower and sesame oils, heat half the mixture in a wok or large frying pan and stir-fry the chicken strips until cooked. This will only take about *3 minutes*. Remove from the pan. Add the remaining oil mixture and stir-fry the carrot for *1 minute*, then add the peppers, mangetout and sweetcorn, constantly tossing and frying over a high heat.

3 Stir the sauce to make sure it is well blended, then pour it into the pan. Bring to the boil and cook for *3–4 minutes*, stirring all the time. Add the noodles and chicken and cook for a further *3 minutes* to heat thoroughly.

4 Pile a generous helping in the centre of 4 warmed plates and sprinkle over the cashew nuts, spring onions and a little of the sauce. Garnish with coriander and serve immediately.

Serves 4

Shredded Chicken with Green Peppers

Preparation time: 10–15 minutes
Cooking time: 10 minutes

- 2 skinless, boneless chicken breasts, cut into thin strips
- 1½ teaspoons salt
- 1 egg white, lightly beaten
- 3 teaspoons cornflour
- 4 tablespoons oil
- 1 spring onion, finely chopped
- 2 slices of fresh root ginger, peeled and finely chopped
- 250 g/8 oz green peppers, cored, deseeded and cut into matchsticks
- 2 tablespoons rice wine or dry sherry

TO GARNISH:

- 1 teaspoon sesame seeds
- spring onion strips
- lime wedges
- sliced red chilli

1 Mix the chicken first with ½ teaspoon of the salt, then the egg white and finally 2 teaspoons of the cornflour.

2 Blend the remaining cornflour in a jug with a little water.

3 Heat a wok until hot. Add the oil and heat, then add the chicken strips and stir-fry over a moderate heat until they turn white, then remove with a slotted spoon and set aside.

4 Increase the heat to high and when the oil is very hot, add the spring onion and ginger to flavour the oil. Add the green peppers and cook, stirring continuously, for *30 seconds*, then return the chicken shreds with the remaining salt and the wine or sherry. Stir-fry for *1 minute*, then add the blended cornflour. Mix well. Serve at once garnished with sesame seeds, spring onion strips, lime wedges and sliced red chilli.

Serves 4

Sesame Chicken

Preparation time: 10 minutes
Cooking time: 20–25 minutes

- 2 egg whites
- 2 tablespoons cornflour
- 2 tablespoons sesame seeds
- ¼ teaspoon salt
- 4 skinless, boneless chicken breasts, cut into thin strips
- 2 teaspoons sesame oil
- oil, for shallow-frying
- coriander sprigs, to garnish

SAUCE:

- 2 tablespoons soy sauce
- 2 tablespoons rice wine or dry sherry
- 1 tablespoon wine vinegar
- 2 teaspoons soft brown sugar
- ½ teaspoon chilli powder, or to taste

1 First prepare the sauce. Mix all the ingredients together in a jug or bowl. Set aside.

2 Lightly beat the egg whites in a shallow dish with the cornflour, sesame seeds and salt. Add the strips of chicken and turn to coat. Set aside.

3 Heat the oil in a wok until hot but not smoking. One at a time, lift the strips of chicken out of the egg-white mixture with a fork and drop into the hot oil. Shallow-fry the chicken in batches for about *3–4 minutes* at a time until golden. Lift out with a slotted spoon and drain on kitchen paper. Keep hot in the oven while shallow-frying the remainder.

4 Pour off all the oil from the wok and wipe it clean with kitchen paper. Return the wok to a moderate heat, pour in the sauce and stir until sizzling. Return the chicken to the wok and toss for *1–2 minutes* or until evenly coated in the sauce. Sprinkle with the sesame oil and serve at once, with a mixed vegetable stir-fry, garnished with a sprig of coriander.

Serves 3–4

Special Photography:
Bill Reavell
Front Jacket Photography:
Bill Reavell
Back Jacket Photography:
Bill Reavell
Additional photographs by:
Octopus Publishing Group
Ltd /Steve Baxter /Laurie Evans
/Graham Kirk /Sandra Lane
/David Loftus /David Munns
/Peter Myers /Alan Newnham
/Philip Webb
Front Jacket Home Economist:
Sunil Vijayakar
Food Preparation/Styling:
Jason Wild at The North Pole,
131 Greenwich High Road,
Greenwich, London
Recipe contribution p48, p75,
by Jason Wild